MONTREAL
BOOK OF
Everything

Everything you wanted to know about
Montreal and were going to ask anyway

Jim Hynes

MACINTYRE PURCELL PUBLISHIN

MacIntyre Purcell Publishing Inc.
1662-#332
Lunenburg, Nova Scotia
B0J 2C0
(902) 640-3350
www.bookofeverything.com
info@bookofeverything.com

Cover photo istockphoto©.
Photos: pages 6, 96, 184 Brendan Murphy, pages.16, 34, 56, 74, 122, 148, 164 istockphoto©.
Cover and Design: Channel Communications Inc.

Printed and bound in Canada

Library and Archives Canada Cataloguing in Publication
Hynes, Jim
Montreal Book of Everything /
Hynes, Jim
ISBN 978-0-9738063-7-3
Montreal (Quebec). 2. Montreal (Quebec)--Miscellanea. I. Title.
FC2947.18.H95 2007   971.4'28
C2007-905133-2

Introduction

I wasn't born in Montreal, but rather in a small town on the city's South Shore. For the past 40 years, though, I have driven over the Champlain Bridge, linking the South Shore and the Eastern Townships beyond it with the island of Montreal, hundreds of times – first as a boy with my dad visiting his family in the city, now with my own family, heading home after spending a day with my parents.

Every time I have made that drive, day or night, summer or winter, I have never failed to be amazed at just how beautiful a city I live in. From the top of the span I can see the small, sprawling bump of a mountain that gives the city its name. I see the powerful St. Lawrence River that made the location so perfect for commerce.

From the bridge I can see rising out of the mostly French East End, the Olympic Stadium, where I danced a goofy, improvised jig in the aisles and sang "Valderi, Valdera" with 50,000 other people, French and English, back in the days when the Expos were packing 'em in. I also see the more Anglo West End and I remember a summer morning pushing my then one-year-old son on the swings in beautiful Westmount Park.

The history books and online archives will tell you about language strife, and a boulevard that divides us both geographically and socio-politically. What they won't tell you is that you can go spelunking in St. Leonard, that the long gone neighborhood called Griffintown used to flood so badly you could row a boat up and down its streets, or that Old Montreal was once destroyed by fire... and that a black slave woman was blamed and executed for it. For that you'll have to consult the Montreal Book of Everything.

I'd like to extend many thanks to all of the contributors and editors. Tim Lehnert lent his time and skills writing many sections of the book with his trademark accuracy and promptness. Paul Waters tackled the culture section with great skill. Samantha Amara, Lynn MacIntyre, Brendan Murphy, and Elizabeth Johnston all performed research and writing. Kelly Inglis deserves special mention for her editing skills and attention to detail.

To know everything about Montreal is a lofty goal, perhaps one that is never attainable. It's a big, complicated city with a long, complicated history. We have had a lot of fun trying. We hope you have as much fun reading about it.

— Jim Hynes

Table of Contents

INTRODUCTION 3

TIMELINE 7
From 2000 Before Present to 2007 . . . First Permanent Settlement . . .
New World . . . St. Lawrence Seaway Opens . . . Montreal USA . . .
Francine Lelievre's Five Sites Providing a Window Into Montreal's Past .
. . Summer Olympics . . . Super City . . .

ESSENTIALS 17
Population Trends . . . Margaret Somerville's Five Things She Loves
About Montreal . . . You Know You're From Montreal When . . .
Ethnic Origins . . . Cussing, a French Lesson . . . David McKnight's Five
Essential Reads . . . Higher Learning . . . Health Care . . .

URBAN GEOGRAPHY 35
Take Me to the River . . . Mount Royal . . . Dinu Bumbaru's Top
Architectural Achievements . . . "Old" Montreal . . . Habitat 67 . . .
Five Things to Do for Free in Montreal . . . Work of Art . . . Two
Wheelin' . . . Tallest Buildings . . . Play it Again . . .

WEATHER AND CLIMATE 57
Monthly Average Temperatures . . . Geeta Nadkarni's Top Five
Weather Tips . . . Ice Storm of '98 . . . Victorian Era Winter Carnivals
. . . Build an Ark . . . Earthquakes . . .

CRIME AND PUNISHMENT 75
Crime Line . . . The Headless Hooker . . . Wide Open Town . . . Wiseguy
Wally's Top Five Underworld Characters . . . Machine Gun Molly . . .
Little Kingpin . . . West End Gang . . . In the Line of Duty . . . Policing
Montreal . . . Brother Andre's Heart . . .

CULTURE 97
An Ancient Art for the Modern World . . . Mordecai Richler . . . Bryan
Demchinsky's Top Five Literary Spots . . . Celine Dion . . . Indie
Paradise . . . Lewis Cohen's Favourite Outdoor Shooting Locations . . .
Revolutionary Art . . . Top Five Sports Teams . . . Ben Weider . . .

ECONOMY 123

Peter Hadekel's Economy Pros and Cons . . . The Bronfmans . . . You
Said How Much? . . . Five Key Sectors in the Economy . . . Pierre
Peladeau . . . Bombardier . . . Needle Trade . . . Shipping News . . .
Downtown . . .

POLITICS 149

Mega City . . . Alan Hustak's Most Memorable Montreal Mayors . . .
Jean Drapeau . . . Property Taxes . . . First Elected Mayor . . . Sticks
and Stones and Trudeau's Bones . . .

THEN AND NOW 165

Five Famous Hotels . . . Population, Then and Now . . . Origins
of Street Names . . . Bibles and Bandages . . . Victoria Dickenson's
Favourite Artifacts at McCord . . . Fire . . . Twentieth Century
Riots . . .

FIRST PEOPLE 185

Creation Story . . . The Great Peace Treaty . . . Chief Donnaconna . .
. Oka Crisis . . . Spiritual Traditions . . . Languages . . . Why the Bear
has a Short Tail . . .

GO AHEAD, TAKE FIVE MORE 197

Luc Robitaille's Five Reasons Why He Loved Playing Hockey In
Montreal . . . Stephen Barry's Five Favourite Performers He Has Shared
A Stage With . . . Jim Hynes' Five Best-Kept Secrets About Montreal .
. . Andra Mccartney's Top Five Lachine Canal Sounds . . . Bernard
Perusse's Five Favourite Concert Venues . . . Paul Waters Five
Favourite Pieces of Street Art . . . Wanda Kaluzny's Five Favourite
Things About Montreal . . . Bill Haugland's 5 Most Memorable Stories
He's Covered . . . Ronald Stewart And William Henson's Five Reasons
Montreal Is Susceptible To Ice Storms

Montreal:

A Timeline

2,000-1,500 Before Present: Archeological evidence suggests that various nomadic peoples occupy the area now known as Montreal.

1535: During his second voyage to the new world, Jacques Cartier explores the Saint Lawrence River, then known as "la Riviere de Canada" and finds the well-populated and well-fortified Iroquoian village of Hochelaga, the present day site of the Island of Montreal.

1611: Having founded Quebec City on the Iroquois settlement of Stadacona, Samuel de Champlain re-explores Hochelaga in an attempt to create a trading post but is fought off by Iroquois. Before leaving, he names nearby Île Sainte-Helene after his wife.

1639: The area's first permanent settlement is created by French tax collector Jerome Le Royer.

1642: Paul de Chomedy de Maisonneuve establishes a mission named Ville-Marie. He erects a wooden cross on Mount Royal. The area becomes central to the fur trade.

1645: Jeanne Mance establishes the Hôtel-Dieu, the first hospital in North America.

1670: The creation of the Hudson Bay Company is the beginning of the conflict between France and England for control of the fur trade profits.

1701: The Great Peace Treaty, between New France and 39 First Nations, is signed in Montreal.

1716: The French begin a 20-year construction of a wall around Montreal.

1721: After a large fire in the city, all subsequent buildings within the city walls must be built using stone.

1759: After defeating the French in Quebec, in what would prove to be the tail end of the Seven Years War, the British army marches towards Montreal.

1760: Montreal is overtaken by the British.

1763: The Treaty of Paris sees control of New France officially handed from France to England, the only exception being the islands of St. Pierre and Miquelon. An influx of Anglophones into the city begins.

1775: The American army marches into the city to solicit participation in the American Revolution.

New World

Born in 1491 in Saint-Malo, France into a family of well-known mariners, Jacques Cartier would continue the family tradition. In 1534, under a commission from the King of France, he set sail to discover a western passage to Asia. What he discovered instead, of course, were parts of North America, in particular the Gulf of St. Lawrence and the St. Lawrence River.

Initial meetings with the First Nations were friendly but upon a second meeting when one of Cartier's boats became surrounded by Natives in canoes, he panicked, ordering his men to shoot off a series of warning shots, despite the Mi'kmaq signs of peace.

A third encounter further diminished relations when Cartier planted a nine-metre cross and took possession of the territory in the name of the king – the St. Lawrence Iroquoians were not amused. In an effort to build a relationship with the natives, he captured two of Iroquois Chief Donnaconna's sons (Taignoagny and Domagaya), and returned to France.

Returning in 1535 and guided by Taignoagny and Domagaya, Cartier became the first European to penetrate the St. Lawrence River. In Stadacona (Quebec City), Native people refused to accompany him further up river, but Cartier found other guides, which this time led him to Hochelaga (Montreal).

When he arrived Hochelaga, Cartier put on his full uniform, and ordered his sailors into formation as he entered what was then an Iroquoian village. After the festivities, the Iroquois brought Cartier to the top of Mount Royal, explaining to him the major waterways. Cartier was convinced he had discovered the passage to Asia.

Although Samuel de Champlain would attempt to establish a fur trading outpost on the island of Montreal in 1611, it wasn't until 1639 that Jérôme Le Royer de La Dauversière obtained the title to the Island of Montreal in the name of the Société de Notre-Dame de Montréal to establish a Roman Catholic mission for evangelizing natives. The settlement was founded a year later.

1779: Montreal merchants create an alliance called the Northwest Company — intended to break the Hudson Bay Company's stronghold on the fur trade.

1817: The Bank of Montreal, Canada's oldest chartered bank, is opened and remains the country's central bank until the creation of the Bank of Canada in 1935.

1821: McGill University is founded.

1821: The Hudson Bay Company and the Northwest Company are merged. The company makes its headquarters in Lachine.

1825: Lachine Canal opens, allowing ships to bypass the Lachine Rapids, turning Montreal into a major port city.

Montreal, USA

In November 1775, Montreal was invaded by American forces. An earlier September attack had been repelled, but the city was poorly defended and surrendered easily to the new American offensive. The Americans were on the verge of declaring their independence, and saw Quebec's Francophones as potential allies in their fight against the British Empire.

Many Montrealers remained neutral in the wake of the occupation, supporting neither the invaders from the south, nor the British who had formally held Canada for only a dozen years. The Americans, led by Benedict Arnold, also tried to take Quebec City, but this effort floundered and they were forced to withdraw. Moreover, representatives of the US Continental Congress, including Ben Franklin, failed to convince Montrealers to lend their support to the cause of revolution. The American forces quit Quebec in the spring of 1776.

1832: Cholera epidemic hits Montreal, causing an estimated 4000 deaths.

1832: Irish immigrant Daniel Tracey, publisher of the pro-democratic paper, *The Vindicator*, is elected to the Legislative Assembly of Canada but dies that same year of cholera.

1832: Montreal is incorporated as a city.

1833: Jacques Viger is chosen as the first mayor of Montreal.

1837-38: Patriotes rebellion (led by Louis-Joseph Papineau) is brutally suppressed.

1844: Montreal becomes the capital of the United Province of Canada.

1849: The Parliament of the United Provinces of Canada is burned down by an Anglo paramilitary organization after the Rebellion Losses Act is passed.

1852: The Great Fire of Montreal destroys 11,000 homes.

1854: Construction begins on the railway-friendly Victoria Bridge, the first to span the St-Lawrence and at the time the longest in the world. It provides the city a vital link in the country's railway system.

1861: Streetcars pulled by horses are introduced.

1917: A 5.3 km tunnel under Mount Royal is completed.

1924: The lights on the new 31.4 m cross on Mount Royal are turned on for the first time.

1931: The Sun Life building in downtown Montreal becomes the largest (square-footage) building in the British Empire.

1934: The Montreal Harbour Bridge, constructed in 1930, is renamed Jacques Cartier Bridge for the 400th anniversary of his visit to the St. Lawrence.

Take 5 FRANCINE LELIEVRE'S FIVE SITES PROVIDING A WINDOW ONTO MONTREAL'S RICH PAST

Francine Lelièvre is the Executive Director of Pointe-à-Callière Museum in Old Montreal. Pointe-à-Callière, the Montréal Museum of Archaeology and History, (www.pacmuseum.qc.ca) was inaugurated in 1992 as part of the celebrations surrounding Montreal's 350th anniversary. Pointe-à-Callière engages in outreach, education, conservation and research on Montreal's archeological and historical heritage. In addition to permanent and temporary exhibits, the museum offers cultural activities, lectures and school programs. Each spring, in partnership with the Université de Montréal, Pointe-à-Callière organizes an Archeological Field School. The digs take place on the actual site where Maisonneuve and Jeanne Mance established the Ville Marie fort and founded Montreal.

1. **Montreal's First Catholic Cemetery.** It's a little known fact that Pointe-à-Callière is home to the city's first Catholic cemetery (1643-1654). The site is a touching memorial to the first European Montrealers. Pointe-à-Callière takes its name from the third Governor of Montreal, Louis-Hector de-Callière, who set up residence there in 1688.

2. **Place Royale's Archeological Crypt.** Since 1979, Place Royale has been the site of a number of archeological digs. These efforts have uncovered fascinating remains of the everyday lives of past Montrealers. Place Royale sits on the remnants of fortifications and buildings erected in the seventeenth, eighteenth, and nineteenth centuries. This was also the site of Montreal's first marketplace, and each August Pointe-à-Callière recreates that lively atmosphere in its week-

1954: Jean Drapeau is elected Mayor and stays in power until 1957. He is then re-elected from 1960 to 1986.

1959: Montreal retires its last streetcar, the fleet now completely replaced by buses.

end long "Public Market" program. The market of centuries ago comes alive as visitors are invited to see, touch and taste historically authentic food. Storytellers, costumed guides and musicians recreate typical scenes from seventeenth century Montreal.

3. **The Old Custom House.** Located on Place Royale near the river, the Custom House was designed by leading Montreal architect John Ostell. This historic Palladian styled building was constructed in 1836-37 and housed Montreal's first customs facility.

4. **The Royal Insurance Building.** The Royal Insurance building reflects the splendor of Montreal, during the second half of the 19th century. Ten years after the building's construction, the Royal Insurance Company relocated to Saint-Jacques Street, the heart of Montreal's financial quarter. The Canadian government acquired the building for customs purposes as John Ostell's Custom House was unable to handle the growth in Montreal's port traffic. The Royal Insurance building was damaged by a fire in 1947, and demolished in 1951. The Pointe-à-Callière Museum's central structure, Éperon, now lies on the foundations of this historic building. Like its predecessor, Éperon has a triangular shape and a tower that surveys the Port of Montreal.

5. **Main Sewer.** On your journey through the museum, you'll cross an impressive arched pipe that runs over what was known as the Little Saint-Pierre River. This sewer line was in use from 1832 until 1989.

1959: The St. Lawrence Seaway opens, allowing ocean-going vessels to travel from the Atlantic Ocean to the Great Lakes.

1962: Construction of Montreal's underground city begins. It remains the largest underground complex in the world.

1966: Montreal Metro (subway) system opens to great fanfare.

1967: Expo 67, erected on Saint Helene's Island and Île Notre-Dame (created with earth displaced from construction of the metro system), is a celebration of "Man and His World." It brings Montreal international recognition.

1968: A new provincial political party, the Parti Québécois, is formed. The party is dedicated to the separation of Quebec from Canada.

1969: The largest student riots in Canadian history occur at Concordia University. Over 200 students occupy a computer lab for two weeks, causing millions of dollars of damage and resulting in nearly 100 arrests.

1970: The FLQ (Front de Liberation du Quebec) kidnaps James Cross and Pierre Laporte, later killing Laporte. During the ensuing "October Crisis" the government, under the direction of Prime Minister Pierre Trudeau, invokes the War Measures Act, a form of martial law.

1972: The 10-day Common Front walkout, which included more than 200,000 public sector workers, ends. It remains the largest labour strike in Canadian history.

1976: Montreal hosts the Summer Olympics.

1976: Parti Québécois wins a majority government. Rene Levesque is elected the new premier of the province.

1977: Bill 101, or the Charter of the French Language, is passed, making French the only official language of the province. While hailed by most Francophones, the law is believed to have caused the exodus of a substantial number of anglophone residents and many businesses.

1980: The first referendum on Quebec sovereignty is held. It is defeated (59.56% to 40.44%).

1990: About 200 Mohawks from the Kanesatake reserve march though Oka protesting plans to expand the village's nine-hole golf course to 18 holes. The Mohawks say the expansion encroaches on their burial ground. As a show of solidarity, residents of the Kahnawake reserve blockade the Mercier Bridge, an important link between Montreal and the South Shore.

1995: Quebec's second referendum, this time spearheaded by Lucien Bouchard, is defeated, though by a razor thin margin (50.58 percent to 49.42 percent).

1998: A massive ice storm cripples the city, leaving many without power for weeks, causing millions of dollars of damage.

2002: Merger of the city of Montreal with the 27 municipalities on the Island creates a new "Super City."

2005: The Olympic Stadium built for the 1976 Summer Olympic Games is finally paid off by taxpayers. Its original projected cost was $130 million but it ended up with a price tag of over $1.5 billion.

2006: A provincial plan (begun in the year 2000) to create a Super-City by merging Montreal area communities turns into a fiasco. After initially being merged, fifteen communities vote to demerge.

Montreal Essentials

Origin of the Name: It's generally accepted that Montreal got its name from the mountain at its centre. The theory is that French explorer Jacques Cartier applied the name "Mont Royal" to the modest peak he ascended when he visited the area in 1535. While the French settlement that was established a century later was initially called Ville Marie (in honour of the Virgin Mary), by the 1700s the name "Montreal" (a contraction of Mont Royal) was commonly used.

Coat of Arms: Adopted in 1833 and modified in 1938. Emblazoned on a silver field is a heraldic cross meant to reflect Christian motives and principles. On the coat of arms are also four emblems: The fleur-de-lis of the Royal House of Bourbon representing the French settlers, the Lancastrian rose for the English component of the city's population, the thistle represents those of Scottish descent; and the Irish shamrock represents early Irish settlers.

Montreal's Motto: *Concordia Salus* (Salvation through harmony).

Official Flag: First displayed in May 1939. The flag is emblazoned with the same heraldic symbols as those of the coat of arms.

Logo: Created in 1981, the logo is shaped like a flower, in which each petal forms the letters V and M, the initials of the name "Ville de Montréal."

Official Flower: Crabapple

Voting Age: 18

Drinking Age: 18

System of measurement: Metric

Incorporated as a city: 1832

Time Zone: Eastern

Area Code: 514

Postal Code Span: H1Y 2G5 – H2A 3A8

Statutory Holidays: Most of Montreal's statutory holidays are the same as those celebrated nationally, with a few exceptions. May's long weekend is called fête de Dollard (after the early garrison commander who led an expedition from the fort of the newly founded town of Ville Marie in 1660 to ambush a much larger force of Iroquois) instead of Victoria Day and June 24th is celebrated only in Quebec as a national

Did you know...

that the customary way to greet friends in Montreal is to kiss them on both cheeks?

holiday known as St. Jean-Baptiste Day (feast day of St. John the Baptist). Other holidays are New Years Day (January 1), Good Friday (the Friday before Easter), Canada Day (July 1), Labour Day (the first Monday in September), Thanksgiving (second Monday in October), Remembrance Day (November 11), Christmas Day (December 25) and Boxing Day (December 26).

POPULATION

Montreal is Quebec's largest city. Montreal's population stood at 1,873,971 in 2006, and that of the Greater Metropolitan Area (GMA) 3,635,733 (2005), making it the second largest metropolitan area in Canada. The GMA is home to more than 45 percent of Québec's residents, and is the second largest French-speaking city in the world.

POPULATION GROWTH

Montreal continues to demonstrate consistent growth in the new millennium with the population expected to grow 3.6 percent by 2011.

POPULATION BY AGE AND SEX

AGE	MALES	FEMALES	TOTAL
0-14	317,140	304,555	621,695
15-24	231,780	229,255	461,035
25-44	534,250	542,565	1,076,815
45-64	475,425	504,930	980,355
65+	204,666	291,005	495,671

Source: Statistics Canada

Did you know...

that in a survey of Canadians by Decima Research, Montreal ranked as the most romantic city in the country?

POPULATION IN PERSPECTIVE (GMA):

- Montreal: 3,635,571
- Calgary: 1,079,310
- Ottawa: 1,130,761
- Toronto: 5,597,000
- Vancouver: 2,187,721
- New York City: 21,976,224

Take 5 MARGARET SOMERVILLE
FIVE THINGS SHE LOVES
ABOUT MONTREAL

Margaret Somerville is Samuel Gale Professor of Law in the faculty of medicine at McGill University. She is the author of a number of books including *The Ethical Canary: Science, Society* and *The Ethical Imagination: Journeys of the Human Spirit*. Somerville has received the Order of Australia and is a fellow of the Royal Society of Canada. In 2003 she became the first recipient of the UNESCO Avicenna Prize for Ethics in Science.

1. **Montreal's Habitat 67:** I live at Habitat 67 and living there has been a large factor in my staying in Montreal. The building is a work of art — a striking schizoid combination of stark, menacing, prison-like concrete and yet the whole is a playful, joyous sculpture. Its setting between the Old Port and the great Fleuve St. Laurent is magical and breathtaking.

2. **McGill University:** There are only a few "Great Universities" and to have stumbled into one of them is one of the major privileges of my life. Like Montreal itself, McGill sits at a crossroads of Europe and America, French and English language and culture, civil and common law, tradition and modernity, religion and secularism, to name just some of the strands that inform and enrich its scholarship and make it particularly relevant to the contemporary world.

POPULATION DENSITY (PEOPLE/KM^2)

- Montreal: 4,438.7
- Edmonton: 1,067.2
- Calgary: 1,279
- Toronto: 3,939.4
- Vancouver: 5,039
- New York City: 10,194.2
- Tokyo: 13,416

Sources: Statistics Canada; World Atlas; US Census.

3. **Montreal as home:** I am a citizen of two of the "best" countries in the world, Australia and Canada, and both Montreal and Sydney feel like "home."

4. **Spring and summer:** It's not just Montrealers who uninhibitedly celebrate the return of the warmth of the sun and, with it, new life, but Montreal itself has a smile on its face throughout spring and summer. It laughs, it plays, it dances, it parties and its pure joy in simply existing is infectious.

5. **Montreal's "Je ne sais quoi":** All of the above are just a small taste of the people, places, experiences, sights, sounds, history, natural beauty, arts, music, architecture, food, style, sophistication and simple elegance that together create the soul of Montreal. It's an old soul – built from First Nations memory beyond time and from almost 400 years of more recent human memory.

- You pronounce it "*Munn-tree-all*," not "*Maaahhhntreal.*"
- You buy your beer and 6/49 tickets at the *dépanneur*.
- To get cash, you stop at the *guichet* (not the ATM or bank machine).
- You drive on the *autoroute* (not the highway or freeway).
- You criticize bad drivers but you are one too.
- Everyone on the street — drivers, pedestrians, cyclists — believe that they are immortal and that you'll stop first.
- You slow way down right before underpasses and overpasses, look for falling debris, then step on the gas . . . hard.
- You've been taking the Metro for years, but have never been able to understand a single word over the PA system after "Attention, Attention . . ."
- You've been to four Stanley Cup parades . . . in a row.
- You've rented something from Dickie Moore.
- You've had to air mail somebody smoked meat.
- You've eaten smoked meat at 4 a.m.
- You know what a five-and-a-half is.
- Hardwood floors are not a big deal.
- You know how to pronounce Pie IX.
- You refer to the Laurentians as "up North."
- You regularly encounter bilingual homeless people.
- You have an aunt who still calls Saint Denis St, "Saint Dennis." And she's never been there.
- Your only fear about jaywalking is getting a ticket.
- You call leaving the bar at 2:30 a.m. "an early night."
- You constantly badmouth Toronto, but have secretly looked into the job market there.
- You cringe when Bob Cole pronounces French hockey player names.
- You call them "running shoes" (not sneakers or tennis shoes).

MONTREALER WHEN . . .

- A coke is a "soft drink" (not pop or soda).
- You were drinking café au lait before it was latté.
- You've taken the #45 bus with the Great Antonio.
- Two feet of snow must have fallen before you consider it too snowy to drive.
- You know the reason why Youppi couldn't give a "high-five."
- You refuse to set foot in the AMC Forum for "moral reasons."
- You were at Rocket Richard's funeral.
- Your dad was at Howie Morenz' funeral.
- You've seen Brother Andre's heart.
- You know where Leonard Cohen's house is.
- Bikers don't scare you anymore.
- You watched Travel Travel and always thought Don MacGowan did good work.
- You know the difference between the SQ, the SAQ and the SAAQ.
- You've graduated high school but have never been to Grade 12.
- You're proud about Pagliaro, Men Without Hats and the Arcade Fire.
- You're a little embarrassed about Corey Hart, Luba and Celine Dion.
- You know you can't order a steak at the Biftek (On St. Laurent).
- You like your pizza "all-dressed" or "plain."
- You still think the coolest ride at La Ronde is "La Pitoune" (the log ride).
- You know there is no pool to be played at the Montreal Pool Room.
- Saying someone is "French from France" is not redundant.
- You've debated the merits of the "spoon guy" who plays on Ste Catherine St.
- Instead of celebrating Canada Day, you spend July 1 moving.

They Said It

FERTILITY RATE:
Estimated at 1.4 children per woman

LIFE EXPECTANCY AT BIRTH
	Quebec	Canada
Male	75.6	77.4
Female	81.4	82.4

AVERAGE AGE
- On the Island: 39.2
- In the GMA: 38.8
- Plateau Mont-Royal: 34.9

UP THERE
The city of Montreal has one of the oldest populations in the metropolitan region (15 percent are 65 and older). Côte St. Luc, the most predominantly Jewish community on the island, has almost four times the national average of people over 80 years old (14 percent).

GIRLS AND BOYS
- Percentage of Montrealers who are male: 49.1
- Female: 50.9

Did you know...

that more than one in four Montrealers is an immigrant?

Take 5 FIVE BOUROUGHS WHERE CULTURAL COMMUNITIES SETTLE MOST

1. **Saint-Laurent:** 48.5% of the population are immigrants
2. **Cote-des-Neiges**, Notre-Dame-de-Grace: 44.9%
3. **Villeray, Saint-Michel**, Parc-Extension: 41.3%
4. **Saint-Leonard:** 38.5%
5. **Cote-Saint-Luc, Hamstead, Montreal-Ouest:** 38.2%

Source: City of Montreal.

LEGAL MARITAL STATUS (POPULATION 15 AND OVER)

At 2.8 marriages for every 1,000 population, Quebec has the lowest marriage rate of anywhere in the country except Nunavut. Quebec's low marriage rate is due partly to the high proportion of cohabitation in this province. In Quebec, 29.8 percent of all couples live common-law, compared to 11.7 percent in the rest of Canada.

ETHNIC ORIGIN

Over 80 ethnic groups are represented in the Metropolitan Montréal area. The largest cultural communities are the following:

- Italian: 163,690
- Irish: 91,560
- English: 86,995
- Scottish: 59,470
- Haitian: 54,485
- Chinese: 44,735
- Greek: 35,385

They Said It

"Let Toronto become Milan. Montréal will always be Rome."
> **– Montreal Mayor Jean Drapeau on Montreal being eclipsed by Toronto as Canada's largest city.**

David McKnight is a former McGill University librarian. He holds an MA in Canadian literature and has worked extensively in the area of 20th Century Canadian Print Culture. Mr. McKnight is presently working on several projects related to the unpublished notebooks and correspondence of Hugh MacLennan.

1. *The Tin Flute (Bonheur d'occasion)* (1947) by Gabrielle Roy. Set in the largely French working class district of St. Henri, it is the bittersweet love story about beautiful shop girl Florentine Lacasse and the ambitious Jean Lévesque. Cast in the shadow of Westmount, the home of Montreal's wealthy Anglophone elite, its looming presence serves as a reminder of the cultural, economic and social disparity that existed in Montreal until recently.

2. *The Watch That Ends the Night* (1959) by Hugh MacLennan. A complex story of love, action and faith set against the intellectual currents of the day (1930s). MacLennan loved Montreal. He published several classic essays about his adopted city: "The Best Loved Street in Canada," "City with Two Souls" and "The Street Car Conductor,"but in "The Watch," MacLennan draws upon his most powerful descriptive gifts to bring the face of Mount Royal alive and present a vivid and sympathetic portrait of Montreal during the Depression.

3. *The Apprenticeship of Duddy Kravitz* (1959) by Mordecai Richler. Duddy Kravitz's dream is to escape Montreal and build a hotel resort in the Laurentians. But what Richler presents in his ground-breaking fourth novel is a vivid and comedic portrait of Jewish life on St. Urbain Street. In what is perhaps one of the most brilliant openings in Canadian fiction, Richler introduces his ambitious and petulant hero, Duddy, through the lens of his classroom antics at Fletcher's Field

High School, modeled on Richler's own Baron Byng High School (long closed). Although much of the world Richler describes in Duddy Kravitz has disappeared, the spirit of Duddy and the St. Urbain Horesman survives as one walks along St. Urbain and over to Wilinsky's Light Lunch for a cherry coke and "special."

4. *Around the Mountain: Scenes from Montreal Life* (1967) by Hugh Hood. In 12 short stories or "scenes," Hood explores daily life in Montreal from the western to eastern tips of the island. He describes familiar Montreal neighborhoods, parks and streets in rich detail. The city comes alive in a series of encounters with a culturally diverse set of characters who are negotiating their aspirations to change and seek a better life. From a pick up hockey game in January; a separatist demonstration on St. Jean Baptiste Day; summer rambles across Mount Royal to midnight explorations of the bustling port, Hood captures the mood of a politically and culturally divided Montreal on the eve of magical Expo 67 and the ominous refrain of Charles De Gaulle's "Vive Le Quebec Libre!"

5. *Crazy About Lili* (2005) by William Weintraub. Almost a decade after publishing his superb social history of Montreal, *City Unique: Montreal Days and Nights in the 1940s and '50s* (1996), documentary filmmaker and author William Weintraub turned his hand to transforming his historical study into a raucous and risqué fictional encounter with the sultry Lili L'Amour, a character based on the infamous Lili St. Cyr, the Swedish-born American burlesque star who entertained audiences with her striptease act in Montreal for two decades. The novel is mostly a send up of McGill University, but more importantly it presents a vivacious portrait of Montreal's burlesque district during its naughty final years.

The Art of Swearing in French

While English-speaking Montrealers curse pretty much the way the rest of the world does, relying heavily on the sexual and scatological, French Montrealers use religious words to shock. Of course, they also employ the old standbys, exclaiming and defaming with words pertaining to body parts and certain bodily functions.

The tradition of taking not only God's name in vain but also some of the scared icons of the Roman Catholic Church, is a long one. In Quebec, the more of these expletives you string together, and the faster you rifle them off, the more powerful the curse. The classic is: "hostie de câlice de tabarnac", literally "host of a chalice of a tabernacle!", but in meaning, basically, "f#ck!ng sh!t g%dd@mm!t!" Then there are the popular "crisse," "ciboire!" "calvaire!" and "sacrament," which work as exclamations or adjectives.

CHRIST WAS CRUCIFIED

Ironically, with the decline of the Church in Quebec, many of Montreal's younger cursers don't even know what they are saying. In fact, in 2006, the Roman Catholic Church in Quebec launched a campaign, complete with large banners hanging from church facades, sensitizing people to the actual meanings of the epithets they routinely hurl with abandon.

But the practice remains popular. Some English Montrealers spontaneously fire off a string of raunchy religious French epithets when they get riled up, especially when drinking, or watching hockey, or both. New Montrealers or those planning a trip to the city might want to get their hands on a copy of the bilingual comedy hit Bon Cop, Bad Cop to bone up on their French cursing.

Filmed in and around Montrreal in 2005, the story of two cops (one Ontario Anglo, one Quebecois) partnered against their wills features a hilarious scene where grizzled Quebecois cop David gives a French swearing lesson to the prim and proper Martin from Toronto…with a tattooed biker goon named Luc Therrien that they have locked in the trunk of David's car helping out.

Take 5 TOP FIVE FRENCH SWEAR WORDS

1. **Tabarnac** Tabernacle: the boxlike receptacle or sanctuary were the Sacramental bread and wine are kept for holy communion.
2. **Hostie** Host: the holy wafer or "body of Christ"
3. **Câlice** Chalice: the cup holding the holy wine: "blood of the lamb"
4. **Ciboire** Ciborium: chalice-like sacramental vessel, usually covered.
5. **Calvaire** Calvary: place outside Jerusalem where Christ was crucified.

WORD ON THE STREET

French in Quebec evolved from 16th Century Norman French, Normandy being home to many of New France's first settlers. Indeed, French citizens encountering French-speaking Montrealers just about anywhere in the world today are quick to recognize "Quebecois."

English Montrealers borrow from francophone co-citoyens, and the French Montrealers from English. Even the most hard core of Anglo rights crusaders say "d'épanneur" (meaning to get you out of a jam) for the corner store. Meanwhile, despite the best efforts of the language cops, they're still ordering "un hot dog all-dress" out in the East End — un "chien chaud" too silly for even the most ardent defenders of *la langue de Molière*.

They Said It

" When I see all the talent in Montreal, I get excited. I feel that this city has a great deal of character. It has a European flair and a North American way of doing things—a combination that is a great source of inspiration for me. "
    – **Kent Nagano, Music Director of the Montréal Symphony Orchestra**

LANGUAGE

In the Greater Montreal Area, 68 percent of the population are native French speakers, 12.5 percent have English as their mother tongue, and 15.5 percent of residents are Allophones (that is a person with non-official language as mother tongue).

With 53 percent of Montrealers fluent in both French and English, the city boasts the largest bilingual population in Canada. By comparison, only 8.5 percent of the population of Toronto is French-English bilingual. Even in Ottawa, the nation's capital, only 40 percent of the population is French-English bilingual.

Twenty percent of Montreal's population is fluent in a third language.

RELIGIOUS AFFILIATION

- Percentage who are Catholic: 74.5%
- Protestant: 10%
- No religious affiliation: 7.6%
- Muslim: 2.9%
- Jewish: 2.6%
- Buddhist: 1.1%
- Hindu: 1.1%
- Other Religions: 0.2%

Source: Statistics Canada.

CHURCH ATTENDANCE

Quebec is overwhelmingly Roman Catholic, but church influence in the affairs of Quebecers continues to wane. Weekly attendance at church has dropped to 20 per cent from 88 per cent in the 1950s, according to Statistics Canada.

Did you know...

that Montreal universities award more than 38,000 degrees annually and account for more than 20 percent of all Master's and doctoral degrees awarded in Canada?

EDUCATION

There are five school boards on the Island of Montreal —three French and two English. In total, there are 124,590 students enrolled in elementary and 98,484 in high school.

HIGHER LEARNING

While Montreal is too big to be considered a college town, it doesn't lack for post secondary students. Among major centres, Montreal is second in North America (after Boston) in university students per capita. There are four major universities in the city: two English language (McGill and Concordia) and two French language (Université de Montreal and l'Université de Quebec à Montreal).

In addition, the École de technologie supérieures, an engineering school that is part of the University of Quebec system, is also located in Montreal, and the University of Sherbrooke has a campus in suburban Longueil. Montreal's universities enroll 170,000 students, approximately the population of metropolitan St. John's, Newfoundland. The Montreal area is also home to sixty-six public and private CEGEPS (collèges d'enseignement général et professionnel) and colleges.

Did you know...

that Montreal has an official moving day—more than 100,000 Montrealers move every year on July 1st? This tradition most likely comes from Scotland, where every 1st of May people were allowed to "break" their lease in order to find a new home. Scottish immigrants continued this tradition when they settled in Québec. Moving day was eventually changed to July 1st so as not to disturb the children's school year.

EUREKA!

Montreal is the university research capital of Canada. The city has over 200 research centres and more than 1,500 institutions that are active in research and development. Approximately 46 percent of Montrealers aged 15 and above have a post-secondary diploma and 22 percent are university graduates.

HEALTHCARE

- Hospitals: 31
- Childhood and Youth Protection Centres: 2
- Local Community Service Centres: 13
- Long-Term Care Facilities: 68
- Rehabilitation Centres: 19
- Number of doctors in Montreal: 2,513

SPORTS

- Hockey (the Montréal Canadiens)
- Football (the Montréal Alouettes)
- Soccer (the Montréal Impact)
- Formula 1 (the Canadian Grand Prix)
- Tennis (the Rogers Cup)
- Basketball (Montreal Royal)

MEDIA

Montreal has four daily newspapers: three in French—*La Presse*, *Le Devoir* and *Le Journal de Montréal*—and one in English called *The Gazette*, which is one of the oldest English language newspapers in North America.

Weblinks

Montreal Gazette
www.canada.com/montrealgazette
The online source for Montreal news, business, sports, entertainment.
The English language paper of record.

Montreal Cam
www.montrealcam.com
MontrealCAM is a network of cameras showing live pictures of Montreal.

Montreal.com
www.montreal.com/tourism/general.html
Almost everything you need to know about Montreal.

Urban Geography

What most people think of as the "history" of Montreal is less than a blink of an eye in geological time. The Montreal region is bordered to the north by the more than one billion year old Laurentian Mountain range. The Montreal plain developed 500 million years ago when land was flooded by the ocean.

Erosion and the collision of tectonic plates over several hundred million years caused continents to shift and land masses to emerge, including the St. Lawrence Lowlands. Mount Royal, the Rigaud and Oka hills west of the city, and the Monteregian Hills such as Mount Saint-Hilaire were born when molten rock rose through the earth's crust, producing very hard rock.

Those hard rock hills partially survived the continual erosion and the comparatively recent major glaciations of the Quaternary (the current geological era which began two million years ago). It was this period that produced the Montreal area as it looks today.

Around 12,000 years ago, the great weight of the last of the glaciers caused the St. Lawrence River Valley to fill with water from the Atlantic, creating the Champlain Sea. The fertile land in the Montreal area is the result of the sediment left by Champlain Sea, which by 9,500 years ago had become a mere lake.

Area: The Island of Montreal measures only 499 km². Viewed from above, the island is surrounded by the St. Lawrence River, des Prairies River and Deux Montagnes Lake.

Elevation: 36 m (118 ft) above sea level.

LATITUDE AND LONGITUDE

Montreal is located at 45° 31' 0" N – 73° 38' 59" W. This puts the city along the same horizontal lines as Venice, Geneva; Lyon, Milan and Belgrade, Yugoslavia, and along the same vertical lines as New York City and Bogota, Colombia.

HERE AND THERE

Montreal is:

- 202 km away from Ottawa
- 556 km from Toronto
- 3,703 km from Vancouver
- 500 km from Boston
- 600 km from New York City
- 1,023 km from Washington, D.C.
- 47 km away from the border with the United States

Source: City of Montreal.

MONTREAL BOASTS

- Over 5,617 km of highway, arteries, collector roads and local streets on the Island of Montreal
- 4,280 km of roads (city of Montreal)
- 700 overpasses, bridges, passageways, retaining walls and pedestrian bridges
- 2,105 intersections with traffic lights (8,800 lights overall)
- 467 km of alleys
- 883 km of railway tracks
- 400 km of bicycle paths and lanes

Take me to the River

It's impossible to underestimate the importance of the St. Lawrence River to Montreal's founding, history and economy. It is part of the city's fabric and mythology: "Suzanne takes you down to her place near the river," sang Leonard Cohen in the 1960s. "You can hear the boats go by." The boats are still going by — the Port of Montreal is Canada's top container port and handles 20 million tonnes of cargo annually, while the Old Port is a leading tourist destination.

The St. Lawrence River stretches nearly 1300 km from Lake Ontario to the Gulf of St. Lawrence in the Atlantic Ocean. In 1535, Jacques Cartier became the first European to navigate the St. Lawrence. His progress was halted by the Lachine Rapids.

Once Montreal was established, the Lachine Rapids would lead to the construction of the eponymous canal in 1825. (Previously, boats had to disgorge their cargo, and then transport it over land until the rapids had been cleared.) The St. Lawrence Seaway, the Montreal section of which was completed in 1959, rendered the Lachine Canal obsolete as a shipping conduit.

As much as the St. Lawrence has been the city's lifeblood, taming it offered early residents a formidable challenge. In the spring, ice in the river would break up, causing flooding. It wasn't until the construction of the Victoria Bridge in 1860 that trains could get on and off the island. Up until that point Montrealers depended solely on ferries.

Montreal has also benefited from its location near the Ottawa and Richelieu rivers. The Ottawa River empties into the St. Lawrence just west of the Island, and the Richelieu runs from Sorel northeast of Montreal south to Lake Champlain on the U.S. side of the border.

For contemporary Montrealers, the river is sometimes a nuisance (commuters stuck on clogged bridges) and often the scene for recreation and leisure, whether it is a family outing at Parc Jean-Drapeau, biking along the river's edge, or crowding the Jacques Cartier Bridge to watch the fireworks competition.

The Mountain

Mount Royal, the park, didn't come into existence until 1876, but the mountain has been there since the beginning. Jacques Cartier climbed it in 1535, and a little more than a century later, Montreal's founder, de Maisonneuve, ascended Mount Royal's slopes and erected a cross.

In the 1840s, the value of Mount Royal as a public space was recognized, and a park proposed; it wasn't until 1872, however, that a million dollars was spent expropriating land and preparing the site. In 1874, Frederick Law Olmstead, who designed New York's Central Park among other major urban parks, was commissioned to plan the park. This was an era of rapid industrialization and urbanization, and Montreal was in step with other major North American cities in creating a large scale urban oasis to protect fast disappearing green space.

Mount Royal is not an imposing summit, but it's impossible to imagine the city without it. The mountain separates downtown from Côte-des-Neiges and Outremont, and Westmount from the Plateau Mont-Royal. The city has taken measures to ensure the mountain continues its prominence by prohibiting buildings taller than it.

It's more or less mandatory for Montrealers to take out-of-town visitors to the observatory near the chalet. The view of downtown Montreal, as well as the river and hills in Montérégie and, on a clear day, Vermont, has inspired generations. Mount Royal is a place for all seasons, and receives about three million visitors yearly.

There are many walking and cross-country ski trails, as well attractions such as Beaver Lake and the 1858 Smith House. In autumn, Mount Royal is an ideal place to enjoy the colorful foliage. The 1998 ice storm dealt the mountain's trees a heavy blow, damaging 140,000 trees and destroying 5,000, but the storm's effects are no longer noticeable.

There is a 55-metre communications tower atop the mountain, but it is the 31.4 m cross that garners the most attention. It was erected by the Saint-Jean-Baptiste Society in 1924, and illuminated on Christmas Eve. The cross's incandescent bulbs were replaced with a fibre optic system in 1992. The cross can be lit in several colors, including purple, which is reserved for the death of the pope.

- 33 km of underground pedestrian passageways
- 19 bridges to access the Island of Montreal
- 7,630 streets
- 109,000 lights and lampposts, 12 of which are gas operated (in Old Montreal)
- 4,500 pedestrian lights
- 1410 km pipes for rainwater
- 1440 km pipes for sanitary water

Source: City of Montreal.

GETTIN' 'ROUND

Downtown lies between Old Montreal and Mount Royal, and the mountain divides the city into a number of residential and commercial quarters. In the central area, a number of lengthy major arteries, both East-West (Sherbrooke, Ste-Catherine, René Lévesque), and North-South (Côte-des-Neiges/Guy, Park/Bleury, St. Laurent, St. Denis, Papineau) are easy guideposts.

In addition to Montreal's natural topography, infrastructure like the port, the Lachine Canal, bridges, railways and rail yards, autoroutes and the airport have had a major impact on Montreal's layout and development.

Boulevard St. Laurent has been the traditional dividing point between the famed "two solitudes." For decades, centuries even, the English were found west of St. Laurent, and the French east. Francophones constitute the overwhelming majority of the population in the eastern part of the city, as well as in Montreal's off-island sub-urbs, and are now found in substantial numbers in former Anglo enclaves such as the West Island, Westmount and N.D.G. Both English and French Montrealers are more bilingual than ever, and while it is true that there are still "English" and "French" areas of the

Did you know...

that the Montreal region is an urban archipelago made up of more than 400 islands?

city, this no longer holds to the extent that it used to.

In the early twentieth century, many immigrants settled in and around the Main in the Plateau Mont-Royal, as well as in a central band of the city heading north. Central Montreal has gentrified considerably, and the formerly ethnic areas around St. Laurent are now home to young professionals, artists and students rather than newcomers.

To the north of the Plateau, Park Extension remains an immigrant precinct, as does Côte-des-Neiges, west of Park Ex. Many of the "ethnics" of fifty or one hundred years ago have now suburbanized; St.-Leonard and Rivière des Prairies are Italian strongholds, Côte-Saint-

Take 5 DINU BUMBARU'S TOP FIVE MONTREAL ARCHITECTURAL ACHEIVEMENTS

Dinu Bumbaru was trained as an architect at the Université de Montréal as well as in architectural conservation in Rome and the United Kingdom. Since 1982, he has worked for Héritage Montréal, an organization founded in 1975 to promote the protection of Greater Montreal's historical, architectural, natural and cultural heritage through education, awareness and advocacy.

1. Restoration of Montreal Savings Bank Ste. Catherine / McGill College (1984): In the age of ATMs, this landmark of commercial architecture was restored in a state-of-the-art project which conserved its interior décor and features.

2. Waterfront planning in Lachine (1988): The sustained initiative of the city of Lachine's Mayor Décarie to acquire property and open up views and public access to the Lac Saint-Louis has created one of the most spectacular public places in the Montreal area. It is now completed by a remarkable collection of large scale art pieces and a truly enjoyable connection to Old Montreal and downtown by the Lachine Canal, its cycle path and reopened waterway.

Luc is overwhelmingly Jewish and Ville Saint-Laurent and South Shore Brossard are veritable suburban United Nations.

Montreal's French working class has traditionally been found in the eastern part of the city. The southwest part of the Island, including St. Henri, Verdun and Point St. Charles, has typically been working class as well, but with a mixed French and English speaking population, a result of the substantial Irish immigration to the area in the 1800s. Many of Montreal's tonier neighborhoods, including Outremont and Westmount, are near downtown, and several others, including the town of Mount Royal and Hampstead, are also close to the city center.

3. Pointe à Callière (1992): Designed by Dan Hanganu, this is a remarkable example of an audaciously modern museum in the heart of Old Montreal, demonstrating that with talent and attention to the environment, architecture can be a form of art in any time. The museum was inaugurated in 1992.

4. Maison du Fier Monde (1996): The conversion of this former public bath (a feature of many of Montreal's older neighbourhoods) to a museum dedicated to telling the story of the working-class families, has contributed to the strong cultural revitalization of one of Montreal's older areas.

5. Unveiling of the historic St. James United Church on Ste. Catherine Street (2005): Built in 1887, this remarkable church had been hidden behind a row of very unarchitectural commercial spaces from the 1930s, some of which have now been partly removed to reveal the church's historic stonework, carvings and architecture.

IN A NAME

French explorer Jacques Cartier named the St. Lawrence on August 10, 1535, feast day of the Deacon Lawrence, who was martyred in Rome in 258. Previous to this, the river had been known Hochelaga River and the Canada River.

"Old" Montreal

Before Old Montreal was old, it was just Montreal. For centuries, the area was the center of Canadian commerce, and the home of many important retail and warehousing operations. By the late 19th century, however, a rapidly expanding population and improved public transportation caused businesses to move away from the river.

The move of retail and commerce northward left Old Montreal a run-down and deserted area by the late 1950s. There were plans, thankfully scuttled, to run an expressway along the waterfront, an urban planning nightmare to which many North American cities have succumbed. The creation of the Viger Commission in 1962 proved vital in preserving the integrity of Old Montreal and curtailing the role of the automobile.

Since the early 1960s, many old structures have been rehabilitated, the Old Port area has been redeveloped, and the Lachine Canal reinvented as a recreation and leisure space. In addition to the many bars, restaurants, and hotels that now dot Old Montreal, there are also a number of fashionable lofts and condos. The recently established Cité Multimédia in an underused industrial area on Old Montreal's western flank is host to firms in the IT and new media fields.

Finally, it should be noted that while by North American standards Old Montreal is certainly old, it's not as old as some people think. Only a handful of buildings remain from the French regime (1642-1760); many have been lost to fire or otherwise destroyed. The cornerstone for Notre-Dame Basilica on Place d'Armes wasn't laid until 1821. Most of the gray stone buildings that give Old Montreal its "French" character were constructed in a time when the city was the pinnacle of what was then known as British North America.

BRANCHING OUT

There are 675,000 trees along streets and in parks and squares in the city of Montreal. The city's public trees are valued at about $700 million, and the most common street trees are the Silver Maple, the Norwegian Maple, the Honey Locust, the Northern Red Ash, the Hackberry, the Siberian Elm and the Little Leaf Linden.

The establishment of Mount Royal and Lafontaine parks in the late 18th and early 19th centuries, as well as the 1931 founding of the Botanical Garden, were recognition of the importance of trees and green spaces in the urban environment. Mount Royal has 108,000 trees alone. There are also 27,000 in Angrignon Park, 10,000 in the Botanical Garden, 17,000 in Jean-Drapeau Park and 2,300 in Lafontaine Park.

PARKS

Montreal has 11 major parks: Angrignon Park, Bellerive Promenade, Saint-Michel Environmental Complex, Des Rapides Park, Jarry Park, Jean-Drapeau Park, La Fontaine Park, Maisonneuve Park, Mount Royal Park, René-Lévesque Park and Ruisseau-de-Montigny Park. Green spaces, gardens and parks account for 10 percent of the land of the Island of Montreal.

Source: City of Montreal.

PARKS AND GREEN SPACES

- Parks and developed green spaces: 882
- Developed area (in acres): 4,535
- Mont-Royal Park (in acres): 500
- Recreational grounds: 522
- Sport grounds: 535

Did you know...

that Gouin Boulevard is the longest street in Montreal, measuring a full 50 km in length?

ANNUAL PLANTINGS
- Flowers: 1,017,000
- Trees: 5,000
- Shrubs: 15,000
- Flowers distributed to citizens: 500,000

Source: City of Montreal.

FOOTPRINT
Average number of hectares used to sustain a Canadian (also known as 'environmental footprint,' a measure of the resource use): 7.25
- Average number of hectares used by a Montrealer: 6.89
- Average number of hectares used by a Vancouverite: 7.31
- Average number of hectares used by a Torontonian: 7.36
- Average number of hectares used by a Calgarian: 9.86

Source: Federation of Canadian Municipalities.

QUALITY OF LIFE
In 2007, Montréal was ranked 22nd out of 215 world cities and third among North American cities in the annual quality of life survey done by Mercer. The results of the survey take into account 39 quality of life determinants, specifically political, social, economic and environmental factors, personal safety and health, education, transportation, etc. From this standpoint, Montreal is among the world's top 25 cities for the fourth consecutive year.

COMMUNITY GARDEN NETWORK
Montreal has the largest community gardening program in Canada, and has been rated one of the three best programs in North America by the American Community Gardening Association. Montreal's network of community gardens brings together 76 garden sites. In total, 6,400 allotments are available for vegetable gardening and 440 more small plots are set aside for young people between the ages of 9 and 14. An estimated 10,000 people, or about 1.5 per cent of the city's adult population, take advantage of this program.

Habitat 67

Take a walk through Old Montreal down to the port and built on a peninsula extending from the north shore of the St. Lawrence toward the two main island Expo 67 sites you'll see a sprawling apartment complex. You really can't miss it. It resembles a pile of shifting boxes, or the inside of a beehive. This is Habitat 67, the only building from Expo 67 still used for its original purpose.

The theme for Expo 67 was "Man and his World," an idea borrowed from the work of French writer and aviator Antoine de Saint-Exupéry. Housing was one of the main themes of Expo 67 and Habitat 67 was commissioned to represent possible futures.

The building includes 354 prefabricated modules which combine to form a three dimensional space structure. The boxes are connected in varying combinations to create 158 residences ranging from 600 to 1,700 square feet. The whole gigantic sculpture incorporates futuristic interiors, links, pedestrian streets and suspended terraces, aerial spaces, skylights of different angles and large plazas.

What is perhaps most amazing is that Habitat 67 was the brainchild of a young Montreal architect named Moshe Safdie, just 26 years old and only three years removed from the McGill architecture program. Safdie had won a scholarship 1959 to examine housing and architecture in the suburbs and downtowns of North American cities.

Safdie recognized an essential paradox among city dwellers. The dream of a home and garden far from the troubles of the city, yet the desire for the entertainment and culture a city offers. This inspired him to design an apartment building that would satisfy both of those desires. Apartments are made up of anywhere from one to eight boxes, depending on the size. Each apartment has a garden and a private entrance.

Safdie's most enduring accomplishment is that he has achieved the architectural equivalent of a home run. The building and Safdie have been praised in both architectural and the urban planning circles, by the public in general, and by its residents.

"Montreal's skyline is defined by its 'mountain,' a hill with attitude known as Mount Royal. It is the city's most prominent natural feature and provides a backdrop to skyscrapers, bridges and the network of city streets. The promenade on the summit offers an exhilarating panorama of the city and the St. Lawrence River below."

– Montreal writer Alan Hustak, *Montreal Then and Now*, 2006.

AN ISLAND CHRONOLOGY

1801: A regular ferry, powered by oarsmen, is established between the South Shore community of Longueuil and Montreal.

1809: John Molson's steamship, "The Accommodation," Canada's first, travels from Montreal to Quebec, taking three days to do so. By 1813 the length of the trip had been cut to less than 24 hours.

1825: The Lachine Canal opens; the idea of a canal had been proposed as early as 1670.

1826: Horse powered boats are introduced to ferry passengers to and from the South Shore.

1856: An explosion aboard the steamer providing ferry service between Montreal and Longueuil kills 50.

1860: Victoria Bridge, linking Montreal to the South Shore, opens. The two km long bridge cost $6.5 million to build and required 2.5 million rivets. The bridge was used for train travel only and was completely enclosed. Passengers noted that it was loud, smelly and vibrated substantially.

1930: The Harbour Bridge, renamed the Jacques Cartier Bridge in 1934, opens and links Montreal to Longueuil.

They Said It

"Montreal is a Saturday city. On Saturdays the whole city begins to tingle. There is celebration in the air, there is frenzy, there is pleasure. Everybody important is out in the streets."

– Don Bell, writing in *Saturday Night at the Bagel Factory and Other Montreal Stories*

Take 5 FIVE THINGS YOU CAN DO FOR FREE IN MONTREAL

High Mass at Notre-Dame Basilica: The building itself is a wonder to behold, but it really comes to life at Sunday morning's 11 a.m. High Mass, when the professional choir and the huge, 7,000-pipe organ are pumping out floor-shaking liturgical music classics.

Tam Tam Jam: Head for the Sir Georges Etienne-Cartier monument on the eastern slope of Mount Royal Park to join the dozens of drummers and/or dancers doing their thing at the world-renowned Tam Tams, where Guatemalan print clothing and dreadlocks are still in style. When the weather is warm enough, say between May and September, the Tam Tams take place every Sunday from noon until the last drummer collapses. Even if you ain't got the rhythm to keep up, the event is great for people watching.

Montreal Museum of Fine Arts: While there is an admission charge for temporary exhibitions, access to the over 33,000 objects that make up the main collection at Canada's oldest museum is free at all times. You'll find Dalis, Rodins and Picassos in the European collection and works by Riopelle, Borduas and the Group of Seven in the Canadian Collection.

Les Jardins Floralies: A legacy of the 1980 Floralies Internationales, these 12 acres of natural wonder put together by some of the finest landscape artists in the world have only grown in beauty since then. Gardens representing France, England, the U.S, Canada and Israel all remain, with perennials, trees and bushes blooming between June and August. Best viewed by pedal boat along a 1.5-kilometre small, winding river.

St. Joseph's Oratory: The world's largest shrine to St. Joseph attracts more than three million visitors per year, the most devout kneeling in prayer on each of the Oratory's 99 steps. Take in the small, 1917 crypt church, the votive candle room, the enormous, domed main church, and the small museum. The museum is dedicated to the life of Oratory founder Brother Andre, whose heart, once stolen and retrieved by police, is preserved in a case there.

1934: The Mercier Bridge between LaSalle and the South Shore opens; a parallel span was added in 1964.

1959: The St. Lawrence Seaway opens.

1962: The Champlain Bridge connecting Verdun to the South Shore opens.

1966: Opening of a Metro tunnel under the St. Lawrence links the Berri terminus to Île Sainte-Hélène and Longueuil.

1967: Louis-Hippolyte-Lafontaine Tunnel Bridge opens. The 6.5 km long structure (1.5 km of which is under the river) consists of a tunnel from Montreal to Île Charron, and then a bridge to the South Shore.

URBAN TRANSPORTATION

The Montreal Transit Commission (known by its French acronym, the STM) is the governing body of the Montreal Transit System. The public transportation system consists of five commuter train lines, four metro (underground) lines and a comprehensive bus system that includes 191 individual routes.

BUS

Consists of 191 bus routes, including 97 with buses that are wheelchair accessible.

Fleet: Includes 662 standard buses, 951 low-floor buses, 93 paratransit minibuses, and two standard minibuses.

On Time: 82.9 percent

Did you know...

that Montreal is the shad fly capital of Canada? Shad flies are harmless insects that live near fresh water, but in May and June, hordes of winged pests invade waterfront terraces.

METRO NETWORK – THE UNDERGOUND
Consists of four lines totaling 66 km of tracks and is served by 65 stations.

Fleet: Includes 759 cars

Kilometres travelled (with passengers): 58,841,161

BUSIEST STATIONS
- Berri-UQAM
- McGill
- Henri-Bourassa
- Guy-Concordia
- Longueuil–Université-de-Sherbrooke

On Time: 98 percent

COMMUTER TRAINS
Municipalities to the west, northwest and southwest of the Island of Montreal are linked to downtown Montreal by five commuter trains. These trains are integrated into the STM bus and metro system.

Take 10 TEN MOST IMPORTANT SYMBOLS IN MONTREAL

1. The Mount Royal cross
2. The Olympic Stadium
3. Place Ville-Marie and its revolving lights
4. Saint Joseph's Oratory on Mount Royal
5. Environment Canada's Biosphere
6. Jacques Cartier Bridge
7. University of Montréal tower
8. The Five Roses neon sign
9. The Orange Julep (on Décarie Boulevard)
10. Guaranteed Milk bottle (on Lucien-L'Allier Street)

Source: Montreal Gazette.

WORK OF ART

Former Montreal Mayor Jean Drapeau considered the building of Montreal underground (metro) to be a work of art. He had a different architect design each station to reflect a different mood and atmosphere. As a result, Montreal is renowned for being one of the pioneers of showcasing art in subway stations. Drapeau envisioned nothing less than a huge underground art gallery.

On a tour of the art in the metro, you can see Claire Sarrazin's butterfly sculpture — called Icare (or Icarus) — at the Parc station and colourful Judith Klein murals at the Jean-Talon station. A stained glass window called L'histoire de la musique à Montréal was installed at the Place-des-Arts Station in 1967. A number of very influential Quebec artists contributed to the underground "art gallery" over the years, including Jean-Paul Mousseau and Marcelle Ferron, members of the art movement Refus Global (Total Refusal).

Today, more than 50 metro stations are decorated with more than 100 works of art, which include avant-garde murals, sculptures, stained-glass windows, frescos and a variety of other media.

TWO WHEELIN'

Montreal is no haven for cyclists – bad roads, harsh climate and aggressive motorists see to that. Still, the city boasts a large number of bike paths, as well as a sizeable and vibrant *velo* culture. Montreal has a total 377 km of bike paths, including bicycle-only trails, street paths with barriers between vehicles and cyclists, and, finally, modest bike lanes in which cyclists share the road with cars.

The Lachine Canal bike path, which stretches 11.5 km from the Old Port to Lac St. Louis in Lachine, is the most traveled bike route in

Did you know...

that Montreal is home to the very first golf club in North America—the Royal Montreal? Founded in 1873 on Mount Royal, the club is now located on Île Bizard in Montreal.

Canada and receives a million visitors yearly. Another popular path in the southwest section of the city is Les Berges, which runs nearly 22 km from the eastern edge of Verdun to Lachine's western border. Montreal is also part of the Route Verte, Quebec's 4,000 km bikeway network that was inaugurated in summer 2007.

The big yearly event for Montreal cyclists is the Tour de l'Île in which 30,000 cyclists bike 50 km around Montreal. A newer event is the carnival Un Tour la Nuit, a 25 km nighttime ride through the Plateau Mont-Royal and Rosemont-Petite-Patrie districts.

The Plateau Mont-Royal has a large number of cyclists and features many well-traveled paths, including ones on St. Urbain, Clark, Rachel, Brebeuf and Berri streets. Montreal cyclists are salivating at the newest bike path on tap: a downtown stretch on De Maisonneuve Boulevard that will provide a straight east-west shot from Berri Street all the way to Westmount.

WATER

The Island of Montreal draws its water from lac Saint-Louis (downstream from the Lachine Rapids), lac des Deux-Montagnes, rivière des Prairies and the St. Lawrence River. Montreal has seven water treatment facilities that supply water to 1.8 million residents, industries, businesses and institutions.

The Atwater and Charles-J-Des Baillets facilities are the largest in Canada, producing 2,917,000 m^3 of water every day, or 800 times the capacity of the new Olympic-size pool at Sainte-Hélène Island. They produce enough water for 1.5 million people. The water is then pumped from the facilities into one of the 14 storage tanks, or sent directly to the 680 km of municipal water mains, then through 4,557 km of arterial pipes to the consumer.

Did you know...

that in 2006, 48,000 square meters of graffiti were removed and 4,650 volunteers contributed to various city-beautifying projects?

Take 5 FIVE TALLEST BUILDINGS
IN MONTREAL

1. **1000 de la Gauchetière (205 m, 51 stories)**
2. **IBM Marathon Building (195 m, 47 stories)**
3. **Stock Exchange Tower (190 m, 47 stories)**
4. **Place Ville-Marie (188 m, 43 stories)**
5. **CIBC Building (187 m, 45 stories)**

Source: City of Montreal.

PLAY IT AGAIN

There are 2,000 playing fields, 150 outdoor swimming pools, 147 multisport fields for basketball, handball, volleyball or ball-hockey, 10 cricket fields, 25 track-and-field facilities, 474 soccer and football fields, 975 baseball fields, 900 outdoor skating rinks, 60 basketball courts, 1,000 tennis courts (two-thirds of which are outdoors), 700 km of cross-country ski trails and 100 indoor skating rinks. Montrealers have access to more than 45 downhill ski runs, 80 golf courses and 90 marinas, all within a 100-km radius of the city. There are more than 100 golf courses in the greater Montreal area.

STAIRCASES

The wrought iron staircase is one of Montreal's most distinctive features. Believe it or not, but the exterior staircase was banned in 1940 because of what the city saw as a deterioration of the quality of workmanship, and because many real estate developers were seen to be sim-

Did you know...

that the Notre-Dame-des-Neiges Cemetery on Mount Royal is Montreal's largest cemetery with an area of 16 million square feet? The cemetery was established in 1854 and is the final resting place for over one million people and more than 10,000 are still buried there every year. Approximately 55 km of routes and pathways crisscross the cemetery.

Take 5 FIVE OF MONTREAL'S MOST ARTFUL CHURCHES

1. **Basilique Notre Dame de Montréal** (110 rue Notre-Dame est.)
2. **St. Patrick's Basilica** (460 boul. René-Lévesque ouest.)
3. **Église St. Léon de Westmount** (4311 boul de Maisonnuve Ouest).
4. **Église de la Visitation** (1847 boul. Gouin est)
5. **Église Madonna de la Difesa** (6810 av. Henri-Julien)

ply adding them on with no due respect to architectural integrity. The ban was lifted in 1994. Staircases are still only allowed to be built on streets where the structures already exist.

FAITH TO MOVE ARTISTS

Montreal is full of great churches built in the day when the city was one of the most pious (at least outwardly) in Christendom. Parishes — even humble working-class ones — competed to have the most magnificent and most lavishly decorated places of worship. And because families were large in those days and Mass attendance virtually universal, many of the churches are large enough to dwarf cathedrals.

The most famous and most stunningly decorated of the city's churches is the Basilique Notre Dame de Montréal — which can sit nearly 9,000 faithfuls for Mass. Keeping the churches stocked with statues, stained-glass windows and paintings provided employment for hundreds of artists and artisans and left Montreal with a priceless heritage. Artists Guido Nincheri and Ozias Leduc and architects Victor Bourgeau and Émile Vanier raised church art and design to heights they've never achieved since in Canada.

Did you know...

that Montreal's first skyscraper at 511 Place d'Armes was built in 1888?

Did you know...

that the cross on Mount Royal was built in 1924 to commemorate the events of December 25th, 1642, when a flood threatened to wash away the early French colony? On January 6, 1643, Paul de Chomedey, Sieur de Maisonneuve, carried a cross by himself to the top of the mountain to give thanks to God for sparing Ville-Marie from the floodwaters. Fibre-optic lighting, installed when Montréal celebrated its 350th anniversary, now illuminates the cross.

MONTREAL'S OLDEST BUILDING

Very few buildings dating from the beginnings of the colony are left in Montreal. Most of the few surviving buildings are religious. The oldest are the Maison Saint-Gabriel (reconstructed in 1698), the towers of the Collège de Montréal (built starting in 1694), and Montreal's oldest building, the Sulpician seminary, built in 1685. Adjacent to Notre-Dame Basilica, the Vieux Séminaire still belongs to the Sulpicians.

Source: City of Montreal.

FORT CITY

Montreal was at one time a fortified city. Construction began in 1722 on a 5.5 metre high stone wall that eventually surrounded the area that is today bounded by Berri, de la Commune, McGill and St. Antoine Streets. The fortifications were gradually removed in the early 1800s. They'd done little good; the city surrendered without a battle in 1760 to the British, and again in 1775 to the Americans.

Did you know...

that one of the figures pictured among the saints and prelates painted on the dome of the Madonna de la Difesa church in Little Italy is Benito Mussolini? (It's there to commemorate the signing of the Concordat that settled the squabble between the Roman Catholic Church and the Italian state over the status of the Pope and the Vatican, one of the Fascists dictators' few lasting accomplishments.)

Weblinks

La Basilique Notre Dame de Montreal

www.basiliquenddm.org

See beautiful photos of the famed church, catch up on current events, find out about the history and more.

Mount Royal

www.lemontroyal.qc.ca

Find detailed maps, discover the principal services and attractions and obtain a copy of the Mount Royal Charter and other documents related to the mountain's protection issues.

Canadian Centre for Architecture

www.cca.qc.ca

A comprehensive site featuring an international research centre and museum devoted to architecture situated in Montreal.

Weather and Climate

Spend a year in Montreal and it's pretty much certain that at some point you will be too hot, too cold or just plain wet. Winters are cold, snowy and long, with daily average temperatures below 0°C in December, January, February and March. Thaws are not uncommon, however, and even in the depths of winter there is a fair amount of sunshine.

Spring comes relatively late, but by May there are hot days and quite a bit of sun. Montreal's summers are warm, often humid, and typically feature substantial amounts of both sunshine and rainfall. Early autumn is cool and crisp and September and October can be exceptionally pleasant, although by November temperatures drop significantly and snow is a distinct possibility.

Montreal is the prototypical Canadian city in terms of weather; it ranks closest to the Canadian average in seventeen weather categories, more than any other center.

CLIMATE AND SETTLEMENT

Montreal's climate may be harsh, but it's milder than most inhabited regions of Quebec. Montreal enjoys frost-free stretches of 140 days or more, and snow is on the ground for only twelve to fifteen weeks yearly, less than in other places in the province.

They Said It

Montreal's plentiful rainfall and warm summers make it ideal for growing a number of crops. Moreover, the Montreal plain is blessed with high quality soil, and is relatively flat. Mount Royal excepted, most of the Island of Montreal is less than 60 meters above sea level. These intertwined geographic, topographic and climatic features made Montreal a natural place for a colonial settlement.

Still, there is no getting around the fact that Montreal is cold in winter. Area waterways would freeze for months at a time, and in the city's early days French ships could visit only once a year. It was not until 1853 that Montreal was linked by rail to an ice-free Atlantic port.

MONTHLY AVERAGE TEMPERATURES (°C)
(AVERAGED OVER A 30 YEAR PERIOD)

Jan	Feb	Mar	Apr	May	Jun	Jul	Aug	Sep	Oct	Nov	Dec
-10.4	-8.9	-2.4	5.7	13.3	17.9	20.9	19.5	14.4	7.9	1.6	-6.6

WEATHER AT A GLANCE

- Rainiest month: August; 92.7 mm rain on average.
- Least rainy month: February; 19.8 mm rain on average.
- Snowiest month: January; 52.5 cm on average.
- Month with greatest average snow depth: February; 18 cm.
- Windiest month: January; 16.6 km average wind speed.
- Sunniest month: July; 274.3 total hours of sunshine.

WEATHER WINNERS

- Coldest day: January 25, 1950: -37.8°C.
- Coldest wind chill day: January 23, 1976: -49.1°C.

Take 5

GEETA NADKARNI'S FIVE THINGS YOU SHOULD KNOW ABOUT SURVIVING MONTREAL'S WEATHER

It goes without saying that Geeta Nadkarni moved to Montreal in the summer. To a girl who'd grown up in Mumbai, India, a city where "winter" meant you could stop sweating for five minutes, -40 sure SOUNDED cold, but the thought of fulfilling her lifelong ambition of owning a trenchcoat overrode any good sense. Ironically, she now works as the weather girl for CBC Television's News at Six in Montreal. You can see her on the CBC roof every evening from 6pm to 7pm, rain, shine, or that famous 40 below.

1. If you're moving to Montreal, a good coat and boots could save your life (or at least your opinion of the city). And it doesn't have to be expensive. I bought my first pair of –40 boots at Yellow for $60, tax included, and my first coat set me back a grand total of $2 at the Salvation Army. It wasn't the chic casually unbuttoned trenchcoat of my dreams. More like a Hasidic man's heavy black wool coat. I looked like a hobo that first winter, but I lived to tell the tale.

2. When it's sunny in winter, it's the opposite of warm: This is a hard truth for someone who grew up in the tropics. A clear blue sky on a winter day seems so inviting when you're indoors and don't know any better. But if the temperature doesn't get you, the wind chill will.

3. The summers are HOT! You'll never run out of things to complain about weather-wise. Plus, the local bugs seem to find non-natives particularly attractive.

4. Catnip is a much better repellent than DEET: I kid you not—like 10 times more effective, according to researchers at Iowa State University. Just get two cups of fresh catnip and put it in three cups of white vinegar. Keep in a dark cupboard for two weeks, shaking once a day. Then strain and transfer to a spray bottle. Apply to self, clothing, patio furniture and other cat lovers. If refrigerated, the mix will stay potent for up to eight months.

5. The best excuse to avoid doing the dishes ever — thunderstorms. You're not supposed to do anything involving running water, even while indoors, during a thunderstorm. It's because lightning might strike an outdoor pipe and the current will travel and electrocute you as you shower/do the dishes. Technically this applies only to severe thunderstorms, but I use it every opportunity I get.

Take 5   TOP FIVE HOTTEST DAYS IN MONTREAL HISTORY (SINCE 1871)

1. August 1, 1975: 37.6°C
2. August 8, 1901: 36.2°C
3. July 1, 1931: 36.1°C
4. July 22, 1955: 35.6°C
5. August 14, 1944: 35.6°C

- Hottest day: August 1, 1975: 37.6 C.
- Largest daily snowfall: March 4, 1971: 43.2 cm.
- Largest daily rainfall: November 8, 1996: 93.5 mm.
- Most powerful wind: March 5, 1964: 161 km/hr.

FEELING HOT, HOT, HOT

Montreal ranks 25th of 100 Canadian centres in the hottest summer category. The highest average afternoon temperature in June, July and August in Montreal is 24.7°C, about the same as Winnipeg, Regina and Peterborough, Ontario. Kamloops, British Columbia is the nation's steamiest place in summer at 27°C, and Prince Rupert B.C. the chilliest at 16°C. Some other Canadian centres' rankings: Windsor (3), Toronto (9), Saskatoon (41), Quebec (45), Halifax (82), Vancouver (91) and St. John's, Newfoundland (98).

Source: Environment Canada.

HERE COMES THE SUN

Given Montreal's ample rain and snow, the city receives a surprising amount of sunshine. Montreal ranks 34 out of 100 Canadian centres in yearly hours of sunshine with 2,029. The prairie provinces are Canada's sunniest region; Medicine Hat, AB ranks number one with 2,513 hours of sunshine yearly. Calgary, Winnipeg, Regina, Saskatoon and Edmonton are all in the top 12 in the Canadian sunshine derby.

Montreal is comparable to 32nd ranked Toronto which gets 2,038 hours sunshine yearly. Montreal gets more sun than Halifax (50), Quebec (74), and St. John's (96). Prince Rupert gets the least sunshine yearly by a wide margin, receiving an average of only 1,229 hours, 60 percent of Montreal's total.

Storm of '98

The Ice Storm of 1998 was a beautiful disaster. Six days of freezing rain in January turned a vast area of eastern Canada (from the Georgian Bay to the Bay of Fundy) into an awe-inspiring, crystalline wonderland. The weight of all that picturesque ice, however, brought down power lines, poles and pylons.

The trouble started when a warm, wet air mass became trapped between two cold air masses, keeping conditions in place for days. Raindrops formed in the warm air, while the cold air layer below was too thin to freeze the drops into snow or ice pellets. Instead the drops froze almost immediately upon impact, forming a smooth layer of ice.

The ice storm ranks as the most severe weather event in Montreal's history. Sidewalks, roads and bridges became impassable. Buildings collapsed, and downtown streets were cordoned off as ice cascaded off skyscrapers in huge blocks. Roads, bridges and autoroutes were closed, and the Metro shut down. On Mount Royal, 140,000 trees were damaged and 5,000 completely destroyed.

Millions of households lost power, and city water was declared unsafe for drinking. It's one thing to lose television privileges for a week, it's another to be without heat and hot water in Montreal in January. A number of people died of carbon monoxide poisoning when they tried to operate barbecues indoors; others were killed from fires, accidents and hypothermia. Thousands of people took refuge in shelters, and many schools were converted into impromptu dorms. The Canadian Armed Forces deployed 12,000 troops in Quebec to help with rescue and clean up efforts.

The area that felt the worst effects of the storm was the "triangle of darkness" just southeast of Montreal. For most Montrealers, the ice storm was an intense ordeal that lasted a week, but in the triangle of darkness, it lasted in some cases more than a month.

IT'S NOT THE HEAT, IT'S THE HUMIDITY

There's a reason Montrealers spend so much time on their balconies in July and August — summers are sticky. Humidity is a trait that Montreal shares with other locales in southern Quebec and southern Ontario. Montreal ranks 13th out of 82 Canadian centres in Humidex days above 30°C with 44.7. Windsor is number one with 67.4, Toronto number nine with 47.6, Quebec number 30 with 30.4, and Calgary number 69 with 6.1. Prince Rupert is last at number 82 with a puny 0.07 score.

Source: Environment Canada.

Montreal's Victorian era Winter Carnivals

During the 1880s, Montreal became famous for its winter carnivals. The highlight was the ice palace, a spectacular fairytale structure with multiple arches and turrets, and a 30 m high central tower. The palace was erected on Dominion Square and illuminated with electric lights. Building the castle was a major enterprise — ice was hauled from the Lachine Canal and then cut into 16,000 m² blocks.

On the final night of the carnival, a "storming of the palace" ceremony was held in which firework toting snowshoers laid siege to the icy castle. Fireworks poured from the sky, and following the snowshoers' capture of the palace from its defenders, there was a torch lit procession to the Mount Royal summit.

The winter carnivals were a huge hit with US tourists, and more than 50,000 Americans came each year to take part in the festivities. It is ironic but prior to staging the first carnival in 1883, a number of Montreal's opinion makers felt it was a bad idea to hold a winter festival. These poor sports believed that the event would discourage immigration by fostering the notion that Montreal winters are cold.

Montreal still celebrates during the chillier months and the family oriented Fête des Neiges de Montréal attracts 200,000 visitors to Parc Jean-Drapeau in late January and early February. There is also the Montreal High Lights Festival, held in late February and early March in Old Montreal. Heavy on arts, culture and entertainment, this festival includes the Nuit Blanche (All-Nighter) in which activities are held throughout the night at a number of venues around the city.

Take 5   TOP FIVE COLDEST DAYS IN MONTREAL HISTORY (SINCE 1871)

1. **January 15, 1957:** -37.8°C
2. **January 4, 1981:** -35.2°C
3. **February 10, 1951:** -35.0°C
4. **February 15, 1943:** -33.9°C
5. **January 3, 1981:** -33.5°C

Source: Environment Canada

HEAT WAVE

Montreal's longest heat wave (a heat wave is defined by Environment Canada as three consecutive days of 30°C or more) was from August 1-10, 2001. Historically, the earliest heat wave in the season was May 17-19, 1962, and the latest was September 8-10, 2002. 1955 was a record year for days with a maximum temperature over 30°C with 33; the average for the period from 1971 to 2000 was 9.

Public health officials warn of a global warming induced increase in heat waves, and the deaths this could cause among Montreal's substantial elderly population. Montreal is vulnerable as it is densely populated in its central area, has an aging housing stock and low air conditioning rates.

Sources: Montreal Gazette; CRIACC; Natural Hazards.

CHILLS

Montreal is known for its cold winters, but the city is warmer than many Canadian centres. Montreal placed 50 out of 100 Canadian locales in Environment Canada's "Coldest Winter" rankings. The lowest average nighttime temperature in December, January and February for Montreal is -13°C, about the same as Ottawa and Moncton, NB, but warmer than Winnipeg and Saskatoon (-20°C), Quebec City (-16°C) and Edmonton (-14°C). Cities substantially warmer than Montreal include Toronto (-9°C), Halifax (-8°C) and Vancouver (1°C).

MONTREAL AND SNOW

Montreal receives its fair share of snow, but ranks only 38th out of 100 Canadian centres in total annual snowfall. Montreal averages 220.5 cm yearly, well behind number one Gander, NL (443.1 cm), number two Corner Brook, NL (421.6 cm) and number three Sept-Îles, QC (412.0). Last is Victoria, BC with a meager 43.8 cm of snowfall annu-

Build an Ark

Montreal has suffered numerous floods over the years. In the 19th century, much of the old town, as well as the working class districts of Griffintown and Point St. Charles would routinely flood. The cause was melting ice in the St. Lawrence River.

Ice would break into large pieces during thaws, and if the slabs jammed, an impromptu dam would form. Water would then overflow the river and flood the city. Watching the ice break up in the St. Lawrence was something of a spectator sport, and Montrealers would line the riverbanks in the spring for this event.

Montreal was hit with notable floods in 1861 and 1869, but the inundation that began on April 14, 1886 is considered the most serious in the city's history. Water levels exceeded one metre, and boats plied city streets, turning Montreal into a North American Venice. Many of the city's wooden sidewalks simply floated away, or were used by intrepid residents as rafts as they poled themselves about town.

The flooding reached as far as Victoria Square (described as "a pond" by one observer), and the foot of Beaver Hall Hill. The Bonaventure Rail Depot also flooded, partially submerging a number of trains. To add to the misery, temperatures dropped and there was a snowstorm. A fire also broke out in a warehouse on William Street and firefighters battled it with frigid water lapping about their waists.

One savvy watch merchant who had lost all of his goods in an 1885 flood took no chances in 1886 – he moved his stock onto elevated platforms chained the sidewalk to the front of his store, and hired a watchman to stand on the floating planks out front and guard the place. A number of enterprising boat owners also set themselves up as water taxis and charged people for rides about the city.

ally. Other snowfall totals and rankings include Quebec City, 315.9 cm (11); Sherbrooke, QC, 294.0 cm (20); Ottawa, 235.7 cm (34); Halifax, 176.4 (52); Calgary, 126.7 (69) and Regina 105.9 (88).

Source: Environment Canada.

SNOW REMOVAL

Montreal gets an average 220 cm of snow every year. Removing and disposing of it, particularly after a major snowstorm, is essential in keeping the city moving. More than 2,000 city employees are in involved in snow removal, and an additional 2,000 workers from private firms are deployed as well.

- Km of Montreal roads needing clearing: 4,200
- Km of Montreal sidewalks needing clearing: 6,300
- Cubic meters of snow disposed of yearly: 13.5 million
- Truckloads disposed of yearly: 450,000
- Number of disposal sites: 26
- 2007 budget for snow removal: $101.9 million

The city of Montreal's snow removal fleet is comprised of more than 2,000 vehicles including:

- 144 spreading trucks
- 326 tracked vehicles
- 154 snowblowers
- 170 tractor-loaders
- 292 graders
- 857 dump trucks

Source: City of Montreal.

Did you know...

that Montreal ranks among the world's coldest major urban centres? Montreal's average January temperature of -10.2°C is slightly colder than that of Moscow, Russia (-9.6), but a little warmer than Minneapolis, Minnesota (-10.6).

Montreal: -8.4°C
New York: 0.9°C
Chicago: -3.7°C
Los Angeles: 14.2°C
Vancouver: 4.8°C

Sources: Cityrating.com; Environment Canada.

DREAMING OF A WHITE CHRISTMAS

The odds are 2 out of 3 that Montreal will have 2 cm or more of snow on Christmas morning. The odds in Toronto are 1 in 3. In the 60s, there was an 80 percent likelihood of a white Christmas in Montreal, and a 60 percent chance in Toronto. Of course, there can be too much of a good thing — on Christmas Day in 1966 Montreal received 32.8 cm of snow.

GET OUT THE SHOVEL

Dubbed 'Montreal's Snowstorm of the Century,' a March 4, 1971 blizzard produced winds of 110 km/h, left 43.2 cm of snow and directly contributed to 17 deaths. Accumulated snow depth on March 12, 1971 was 102 cm, and the city removed 500,000 truckloads of the white stuff. A close second to the 1971 dump was what one might call the 'Storm of the Next Century,' a December 16, 2005 snowfall of 41.2 cm. Near white-out conditions prevailed, and many people simply aban-

Did you know...

that snow was being shoveled right up until game time to clear the stands for the first home game in Montreal Expos history? The playing field for the April 14, 1969 match resembled a "flooded pasture," according to the *Washington Post*.

Take 5 AVERAGE DECEMBER TEMPERATURES IN FIVE CITIES AROUND THE WORLD

1. **Montreal:** -6.3°C
2. **Buenos Aries, Argentina:** 22°C
3. **Helsinki, Finland:** -3°C
4. **Hong Kong:** 17°C
5. **Cape Town, South Africa:** 19°C

Source: Environment Canada; Euroweather.

doned their vehicles. The city deployed 1,500 workers during the storm, and over 200 flights were cancelled.

Sources: Environment Canada; CBC.

STAY OFF THE ROADS

A February 2006 storm whipped through much of Southern Quebec and Southern Ontario bringing rain, freezing rain and snow, and causing 140,000 Quebecers to lose power. The storm produced a 60-car pile-up near Joliette, 75 km northeast of Montreal, causing one death and multiple injuries. Extremely high winds caused a number of large trucks to tip over, and resulted in the derailment of a freight train in the LaSalle area of Montreal. A stretch of Highway 40 in Montreal was closed when glass shattered in a building on nearby Crémazie Boulevard and rained down onto the expressway.

They Said It

"A few acres of snow." – Translation of Voltaire's dismissive evaluation of New France as *"quelques arpents de neige."*
– The French philosopher was writing at the time of the Seven Years' War (1756-63). The treaty ending the conflict specified that France cede its North American colony (the small fishing islands of Saint Pierre and Miquelon excepted) to the British.

Take 5 THE WEATHER ON 5 DAYS IN RECENT MONTREAL HISTORY

1. **Closing ceremonies of the 1976 Olympics.** August 1, 1976, 8pm: 17.2°C; mainly clear.
2. **1980 Quebec sovereignty referendum.** May 20, 12pm: 19.2°C; clear.
3. **École Polytechnique massacre in which 14 women were killed.** December 6, 1989, 5:10pm: - 1°C; freezing drizzle and fog.
4. **1995 Quebec sovereignty referendum.** October 30, 12pm: 2.8°C; mostly cloudy.
5. **First minute of the new millennium January 1, 2000.** 12:01am: -9.3°C; snow.

All temperatures reported at Pierre Elliott Trudeau International Airport (Dorval)
Source: Environment Canada; Euroweather.

RAIN CHECK

Out of the 100 most populated cities and towns in Canada, Montreal is ranked the 45th wettest. It's ranked 37th for the highest number of wet days and 46th for the highest number of very wet days (over 25 mm).

FLASH FLOOD

One of the most intense periods of rain in recent Montreal history occurred on July 14, 1987 when the city was hit with 100 mm of rain. 86 mm of rain fell in a one-hour period in downtown Montreal. The deluge caused flooding in over 40,000 Montreal homes, and 350,000 dwellings lost power.

Moreover, two people were killed — one by electrocution, the

Did you know...

that Montreal was hit with a major ice storm in February 1961? While not as serious as the notorious 1998 storm, the '61 freeze produced wind gusts reaching 130km/hr and dumped 30 mm of freezing rain on the Montreal region.

AVERAGE YEARLY RAINFALL FOR FIVE CANADIAN CITIES

(RANKING OUT OF 100 CANADIAN PLACES IN AVERAGE RAINFALL)

1. **Halifax, 1254.3 mm** (6)
2. **Vancouver, 1154.7** (9)
3. **Montreal, 760.0** (45)
4. **Toronto, 684.6** (58)
5. **Saskatoon, 265.2** (95)

Source: Environment Canada

other when he was unable to exit from his submerged car. Particularly hard hit were the autoroutes, notably the Decarie Expressway, which became a canal of sorts as the water level hit 3.6 meters, resulting in the abandonment of 300 cars. Those taking public transportation didn't fare much better — the Metro was closed when water flooded the tracks. Total damage from the brief storm was estimated at $40 million.

FLASH, CRACK, BOOM

Montreal is the top city in Quebec for lightning flashes with 112 per 100 square km. Windsor, Ontario leads Canada with 251, followed by Toronto with 200. High incidence of lightning is primarily a Southern Ontario phenomena; Montreal is 7th nationwide and Saskatoon 6th, but the top 5 are all in the Toronto-Windsor corridor.

Did you know...

that in 2006 the Montreal Stock Exchange, in collaboration with the Chicago Climate Exchange, established the Montreal Climate Exchange, Canada's first. The Exchange, when fully operational, will allow for trading in greenhouse gas emission credits and similar transactions.

"I rode around in a boat in the hotel dining room and out of the great front door on McGill Street and over to Craig and Notre Dame Streets, and watched the men passing out loaves of bread to the people in the second-storey windows."

– Recollection of an Albion Hotel guest at the time of Montreal's 1886 flood.

SMOG GETS IN YOUR EYES

Montreal isn't Cairo, but it is the worst city in Quebec for air quality. In 2005, Montreal registered 67 poor air quality days, indicating elevated readings of ozone and fine particulate matter. By way of comparison, Quebec City recorded 33 such smoggy days in 2005, while the Saguenay Lac St. Jean region had Quebec's cleanest air with only nine high smog days.

Source: Government of Quebec.

Did you know...

the 1998 ice storm, the brunt of which fell on Southwestern Quebec, was the second most expensive environmental disaster in Canadian history? The bill for the ice storm was estimated at $4.2 billion. Canada's most expensive climate related disaster was the 2001-02 drought, which affected much of the nation and cost five billion dollars. The 1996 Saguenay floods ranked as the fifth costliest weather event with a one billion dollar economic toll.

Take 5 TOP FIVE RAINIEST DAYS IN MONTREAL HISTORY (SINCE 1871)

1. **July 14, 1987:** 100.2 mm
2. **July 5, 1958:** 90.4 mm
3. **July 20, 1880:** 87.6 mm
4. **October 06, 1932:** 86.1 mm
5. **August 29, 1892:** 85.3 mm

Source: Environment Canada

YAR SHE BLOWS....

Montreal is the 35th windiest out of 82 Canadian cities. Montreal's average wind speed is 14.3 km/hr. Some areas, however, can be exceptionally breezy, including spots along the St. Lawrence River, the Lachine Canal, and downtown where skyscrapers on de Maisonneuve and René Lévesque Boulevards have created wind tunnels.

St. John's, NL is the country's windiest city, while Kelowna, BC has the most placid breezes. Montreal is less windy than Regina, which is ranked number 5, Charlottetown, PEI (10) and Hamilton (11). Calgary (27) and Toronto (32) are comparable to Montreal, while less windy cities include Quebec (46), Edmonton (61) and Vancouver (64). Sherbrooke, QC, just 150 km east of Montreal, ranks 79 out of 82 Canadian centres with an average highest wind speed of only 9.2 km/hr.

Source: Environment Canada.

Did you know...

that hail poses a major danger to crops in Montreal and Southwestern Quebec? Two Montreal-area hail storms in the mid-1980s caused substantial losses. A May 29, 1986 storm produced hailstones as big as baseballs and resulted in $90 million damage. Exactly one year later, another hailstorm caused $125 million in damage.

EARTHQUAKES

Montreal is not in great danger from earthquakes; however, there is an "earthquake corridor" that runs from the Ottawa Valley to the area south of Montreal. Considered a "zone of weakness" rather than an "active interplate region," such as the San Francisco Bay Area and Vancouver, Southern Quebec is nevertheless susceptible to minor shakes.

In January 2006, an earthquake of magnitude 4.2 occurred just east of Huntingdon, Quebec, not far from the New York State border. Montreal's most serious earthquake was in 1732 when a substantial jolt damaged 300 houses and caused a fire that destroyed another 185. The quake resulted in a number of injuries as well as one death, and produced considerable panic and anxiety in the small colonial town.

Sources: CBC; Natural Resources Canada.

Did you know...

that Environment Canada's supercomputer debuted in 2004 and is housed in Dorval, Quebec, 20 km west of downtown Montreal?

Weblinks

National Climate Data and Information Archive

www.climate.weatheroffice.ec.gc.ca/Welcome_e.html

Planning a summer street party or an autumn wedding and wondering if the weather is likely to cooperate? Curious about the weather on the day you were born? Trying to decide in what month to take that camping trip? Environment Canada has got years of weather data online. Pick a location and check out monthly averages, or pull up stats for specific dates going back to 1840.

Canada's Top Ten Weather Stories

www.msc-smc.ec.gc.ca/media/top10/index_e.html

Annually, Canada's superstar climatologist David Phillips recaps and ranks the year's notable weather events. His perspective extends beyond summary of the severity of each event to comment on such topics as the impact it had on Canadians and the economy.

Top Weather Events of the 20th Century

www.msc-smc.ec.gc.ca/media/top10/century_e.html

In 2000, Canadians across the country helped Environment Canada select the most notable weather events in Canada of the past 100 years.

Crime and Punishment

CRIME LINE

1680: Montreal subordinate governor Francois Perrot uses beatings and intimidation to control the fur trade and enrich himself.

1690: Jean Haude Heart is convicted of murdering Francois Pougnet. In the first death penalty execution in Montreal history, Heart's hand is cut off in front of his victim's house. He also receives six sharp blows on the legs, thighs and arms and then is "broken on the wheel" until dead.

1734: Suspected arsonist, slave Marie-Joseph Angelique, is tortured until she confesses, and is then hanged.

1752: Jean-Baptiste Bélisle, who robbed and murdered a Montreal couple, is "broken alive" for his crime.

1785: Three men convicted of stealing a mill from John Molson's brewery are hanged.

1803: Convicted murderer Ignace Vaillancourt is sentenced to be hanged, "dissected and anatomized."

1803: B. Clement is hanged for allegedly stealing a cow.

1838-39: Twelve men who took part in the Lower Canada Rebellion of 1837, including leaders Joseph Cardinal, Joseph Duquet and Francois-Marie-Thomas Chevalier de Lorimier, are hanged for treason at the Pied-du-Courant prison.

1861: Spectators riot when one of two men scheduled to be hanged receives a last-minute reprieve.

1871: Johan Ingebretson, aka John Lee, is hanged for robbing and murdering his landlady in Montreal's Griffintown neighborhood.

1887: Two Montreal police detectives are convicted of burglary.

1910: Thirty-seven year-old Timothy Candy is hanged for shooting two Montreal police officers. The officers were arresting him for stealing a pair of rubber boots.

The Headless Hooker

Now virtually disappeared as a community, Griffintown was a Montreal industrial slum inhabited mainly by poor Irish immigrants, most of whom worked building the nearby Lachine Canal and Victoria Bridge. In 1879, after a night of carousing with fellow prostitute Susan Kennedy and a male acquaintance at a house on the corner of William and Murray streets, Mary Gallagher was killed and beheaded — reportedly by the inebriated and jealous Kennedy, who, legend says, deposited Gallagher's head into a bucket in her kitchen.

Kennedy was convicted of murder, while the male friend, a customer common to both women, was acquitted. Griffintown legend has it that Mary Gallagher's ghost returns to haunt her old neighbourhood every seven years in search of her head.

Wide Open Town

In 1881, Mark Twain said that you couldn't throw a brick in Montreal without breaking a church window. And in post-war Montreal, things were not all that different. By night, however, the city shed its pious cloak and transformed itself into Sin City.

The city, particularly the area near the intersection of Ste. Catherine St. and St. Laurent Blvd., was overrun with gambling dens and brothels. Despite church grumblings, it remained that way for decades, due in part to police and political corruption. Police raids were staged. Stooges who were hauled in were fined paltry sums and by nightfall, it would be business as usual. The house at 312 Ontario St. had become famous across Canada for the quality of its prostitutes, and some of the gaming houses in the city were taking in $75,000 an hour.

In 1946, civic authorities only reacted to the situation after the Canadian military threatened to make Montreal off-limits to servicemen. (Many of Canada's enlisted men would come back with empty pockets and syphilis.) In 1946, Montreal Police Chief Fernand Dufresne fired the leader of the city's Morality Squad (the seventh time in 10 years) and replaced him with an unknown lawyer, the crusading Pacifique Plante.

Soon, big names began to fall, like gambling kingpin Harry Ship, the owner of several gambling houses and nightclubs like Chez Paree. Plante, however, had stepped on too many toes and was eventually forced from office. Vice flourished again until he returned with a vengeance with a series of newspaper articles chronicling corruption. The articles helped launch an official probe conducted by Justice Francois Caron.

Together with a young dynamic lawyer named Jean Drapeau, Plante exposed the city's dirty laundry for all to see. After hearing 374 witnesses over 358 sessions, Justice Caron read his judgment in 1953, announcing the firing of 19 police officers, including Police Director Alfred Langlois. The scandal cost Montreal Mayor Camilien Houde the next election. The new mayor turned out to be the candidate for the Civic Action League, Jean Drapeau.

1924: On October 24, mobster Tony Frank and three associates, including a former Montreal police officer, are hanged for killing bank truck driver Henri Cléroux and stealing $142,388.

1924: Future Mafia Godfather Vincenzo "Vic the Egg" Cotroni arrives in Montreal from Calabria, Italy at the age of 14.

Take 5 — WISEGUY WALLY'S TOP FIVE UNDERWORLD CHARACTERS

Wiseguy Wally is the nom de plume of Gary Francoeur, who the *Montreal Mirror* in 2003 called the self-appointed "online archivist of local organized crime clans." He owns and runs Wiseguy Wally's MontrealMafia.com and is a frequent contributor of Montreal stories to a number of popular crime Internet sites.

1. **Donald Lavoie:** Chicoutimi-born Daniel Lavoie participated in at least 27 underworld murders during his time as a henchman for Montreal's fearsome Clan Dubois. After learning that his employers had placed a contract on his head, Lavoie became an informant, helping police put away many of his former associates.

2. **Danny Pelansky:** Known by associates as "One-a-Day" Pelansky because of his dedication to breaking-and-entering, Danny Pelansky plied his illicit trade in the city's west end throughout the 1960s. He also dabbled in numerous moneymaking schemes, including a vending machine operation that was so lucrative that armoured trucks picked the profits up at his Dollard des Ormeaux home. On July 11, 1970, following three failed attempts on his life, including one where he was shot three times and thrown in the trunk of a car, his luck ran out. "One-a-Day" was killed when a bomb planted under the driver's seat of his Buick Wildcat exploded.

3. **Yves "Apache" Trudeau:** Standing five-foot-six and weighing just 135 pounds, "Apache" Trudeau was not the prototypical biker, but that didn't stop him from becoming the Hell's Angels' most prolific

1930: Paul Bélisle is convicted of murder and hanged in the shooting death of Montreal police constable Dollard Pelletier.

1935: Mrs. Thomasina Sarao and two male accomplices are hanged for the murder of her husband, Nicholas Sarao. At her March 28 execution, Mrs. Sarao is decapitated after hangman Arthur Ellis miscalculates her weight. She weighed 32 pounds more than what he had been told.

killer. Between 1973 and 1985, Trudeau carried out 43 contract killings for the Angels and other gangs. Trudeau eventually grew too wild and his biker brothers marked him for death. While five members of the Hell's Angels North Chapter he belonged to were lured to a secret meeting and gunned down by the gang, Trudeau avoided the massacre by entering a rehab centre. He was spared, and eventually turned into a police informant and testified against his fellow bikers.

4. **Paolo Violi:** Seen by many as the heir to Vic Cotroni's throne atop the Montreal Mafia, Violi treated St. Leonard as his own personal fiefdom, controlling all criminal rackets in the largely Italian neighbourhood. Sicilian members of the family resented the Calabrian-born leader and a war soon erupted between the two factions. The ensuing conflict would claim the lives of a dozen mobsters, including two of Violi's brothers. On January 22, 1978, while he was playing cards with friends in a Jean Talon St. cafe, gunmen hiding inside the establishment shot him dead.

5. **Frank Peter "Dunie" Ryan:** As top dog of the West End Gang, Frank "Dunie" Ryan acted as Montreal's primary drug broker, commanding a near monopoly of all cocaine and hashish flowing into the city during the 1970s and early 80s. Incredibly, Ryan was said to have amassed a fortune of between $50 to $100 million, money he supposedly buried at different spots around the city. On November 13, 1984, Ryan was gunned down by a pair of small time hoods. Intending to scare him into divulging where he had stashed his ill-gotten gains, they ended up killing him after he fought back. He was 42.

1938: All executions in Quebec are now carried out at Montreal's Bordeaux prison.

1946: Former crime boss Harry Davis is gunned down by a rival. Over 5,000 people attend his funeral.

1950: The Caron inquiry into police and political corruption in Montreal begins.

1951: Joseph-Albert Guay is hanged at Bordeaux prison for the 1949 bombing of an airplane that kills 23 people, including his wife. He had wanted to marry his mistress.

1953: Marguerite Pitre, an accomplice of Joseph-Albert Guay in the 1949 bombing of an airplane, is hanged at Bordeaux prison. She is the last woman executed in Canada.

1953: The Caron inquiry ends on April 2. Police Director Albert Langlois is fired and dozens are punished as a result of its findings.

Slave Arsonist

On April 10, 1734, Marie-Joseph Angelique, a 29-year-old black slave of Portuguese origin, was accused of setting fire to her owner's home. The fire she was accused of lighting spread, engulfing and destroying the home as well as 45 other buildings, including a convent and the Hotel-Dieu hospital in what is now Old Montreal.

Even though no lives were lost, her punishment was swift and severe. Captured and tortured until she confessed, Angelique was led about town on a garbage cart with a rope around her neck. Wearing a long white shirt with the word "incendiare" (arsonist) written at the front and back, she was taken to the gallows and hung, and later, for good measure, burned.

1953: Bonanno crime family under-boss Carmine Galente arrives in Montreal to supervise the Mafia's illegal gambling operations.

1954: Police raid the home of alleged gangster Frank Petrula, finding $18,000 in cash and records of bribes made to journalists and politicians.

1956: Mining prospector Wilbert Coffin is hanged at Bordeaux prison for the murder of three American tourists. His family and other supporters proclaim his innocence and continue to try and clear his name.

1960: On March 11, at Bordeaux prison, Ernest Côté is hanged for shooting a bank manager during a robbery. It is the last execution in Quebec.

Machine Gun Molly

The media gave her a flashy nickname and a 2004 Quebec film was made about her, but Monica Proietti's life was anything but glamorous. Born into a dirt-poor family in 1939, Proietti grew up on the mean streets of Montreal's East End. By the age of 13, she worked as a prostitute, and before she was 18 she was married to Scottish gangster Anthony Smith.

When Smith was deported from Canada in 1962, Proietti became involved with bank robber Viateur Tessier. When Tessier was sent to jail for 15 years, a broke and desperate Proietti worked as the getaway driver for another gang of bank robbers. Before long, Proietti was in charge, and though she dressed like a man during the heists, both the English and French media were calling her Machine Gun Molly, or Monica la Mitraille.

On September 19, 1967, the police caught up with Proietti after she and two of her gang members robbed a Montreal North Branch of the Caisses Populaires of $3,000. She was gunned down by a Montreal police officer during a shootout that followed a high-speed car chase. Proietti was suspected of robbing over 20 banks. A mother of three, she died at age 27.

1963: A bomb planted in a Westmount mailbox by Front de Libération du Quebec (FLQ) terrorists explodes, maiming army explosives expert Sergeant Major W. R. Leja.

1964: Montreal underworld figure Lucien Rivard is arrested for drug trafficking in Texas and extradited to Canada.

1965: Lucien Rivard escapes from Bordeaux prison on March 2, but is recaptured 4 months later.

1967: Montreal police gun down bank robber Monica Proietti, aka Machine Gun Molly.

1969: FLQ bombs injure 27 at the Montreal Stock Exchange.

The Little Kingpin

Harry Davis was the kingpin of the Montreal underworld in the 1920s and '30s, and was famous for the number of police and municipal officials on his "payroll." The diminutive Davis and his large gang controlled the city's drug, prostitution and gambling trades from his Stanley St. headquarters.

He also owned the popular Frolics nightclub, the home away from home to the city's leading hoodlums. Convicted of drug smuggling in 1933 on the testimony of one of his underlings, Davis was sentenced to 14 years (and 10 strokes of the lash). His influenced waned during his imprisonment and by the time of his release in 1945, the Montreal underworld was under the control of the Italian Mafia and Vic "the Egg" Cotroni.

Still running gambling houses and other rackets, Davis narrowly escaped a bombing attempt on his life on July 14, 1946. Fourteen days later, he was shot to death by a disgruntled small-time gangster named Louis Bercovitch. Approximately 5,000 Montrealers turned out for his funeral.

1970: FLQ terrorists kidnap British Diplomat James Cross on October 5, setting off the October Crisis. Quebec Vice-Premier and Minister of Labour Pierre Laporte is kidnapped from his St. Lambert home five days later. On October 15, Quebec Premier Robert Bourassa asks the federal government to have the Canadian army help restore law and order in the province. The following day, Canadian Prime Minster Pierre Trudeau invokes the War Measures Act to help round up suspected FLQ members. On October 17, the FLQ announces that Pierre Laporte has been executed. His body is later found in the trunk of a car at the St. Hubert airport.

All in The Family: Le Clan Dubois

In the 1960s and '70s, the fearsome French-Canadian Clan Dubois (or Dubois Gang) was the most ruthless and successful criminal group in Montreal outside of the Mafia. Hailing from the rough St. Henri neighbourhood in southwest Montreal, the nine Dubois brothers were the driving force behind a powerful criminal organization that was some 200 strong.

Headed by eldest brother Claude, the Dubois Gang ran drugs, strippers, protection rackets and engaged in loan-sharking and armed robbery. Those who refused protection, or tried selling drugs on the Dubois' territory, were dealt with mercilessly. In 1974, the Dubois' became engaged in the brutal "War of the West" with the smaller McSween Gang over a key piece of West End drug turf.

Nine people, including McSween leader Jacques McSween, were killed. The war ended with a bang on February 14, 1975, when gunmen burst into a south shore disco frequented by the McSween Gang, killing four, including new McSween leader Roger "le Moineau" Létourneau and wounding several others. It was Montreal's own Valentine's Day Massacre.

1970: Following a police raid, FLQ Chenier cell member Pierre Lortie is arrested on November 6 and charged with the murder of Pierre Laporte. In exchange for the safe passage to Cuba for five of its members, the FLQ frees hostage James Cross on December 3. On December 27, the three remaining members of the Chenier cell are arrested and charged with the murder of Pierre Laporte.

1973: Brother Andre's heart is stolen from St. Joseph's Oratory.

1975: Hit men working for the Dubois brothers kill four and wound several others at a hangout of their rivals, the McSween Gang.

1978: Mafia Godfather Paolo Violi is gunned down at his ice cream and coffee bar.

1980: NHL President Clarence Campbell and his business partner Gordon Brown are found guilty of bribery in the Dorval airport "Sky Shops" affair. Each is fined $25,000 and serve a one-day jail sentence.

1980: Montreal police find $700,000 in cash and hashish valued at $9 million in a single drug raid.

1984: West End Gang leader Frank "Dunie" Ryan is murdered in a St. Jacques St. motel.

1985: Five members of the Hell's Angels Laval chapter are murdered by their "brothers" from other Quebec chapters.

1989: On December 6, Marc Lepine kills 14 female engineering students and injures 14 other people at École Polytechnique.

1992: Disgruntled professor Valery Fabrikant kills four colleagues and injures one other at Concordia University.

1995: Montreal police, Sûreté du Quebec and the RCMP form the Wolverine Task Force to combat biker crime.

The West End Gang

With roots going back to Montreal Irish criminal gangs at the beginning of the 20th century, the West End Gang today is part of the unholy triumvirate with the Montreal Mafia and biker gangs sometimes called the Consortium. Unlike those organizations, it has no single leader but is a collection of related groups lead by captains.

The group has a long history committing bank break-ins, safe-cracking jobs, armed robberies and drug trafficking. Thanks to its strong presence at the Port of Montreal, the West End Gang has controlled the importing of massive quantities of narcotics into Montreal since the mid-1970s.

Some of the more infamous West End Gang members of recent history include Frank "Dunie" Ryan, a high school dropout turned bank robber who was allegedly worth between $50 and $100 million when he was murdered in 1984. Ryan's business was taken over by his right-hand man, Allan "the Weasel" Ross, who avenged his boss' murder before being arrested and imprisoned on murder and drug charges in Florida in the late 1990s.

Thought to control the Port of Montreal, the Matticks brothers, Richard and Gerald, beat a variety of charges before they were finally sent to prison for hijacking a truck in 1992. The brothers and five accomplices were arrested again in 1994 when police seized 26.5 tons of hashish at the Port of Montreal. In what became known as the Matticks Affair, however, the case against them was thrown out of court when it was discovered that Sûrêté du Quebec officers had planted some of the evidence against them.

The police finally caught up with Gerald Matticks in 2001 when he was arrested in a series of raids against the Hells Angels and their associates. He was accused of being the biker club's chief source of hashish and police evidence showed that he had smuggled over 33,000 kilograms of hashish and 250 kilograms of cocaine in a single year. Matticks plead guilty and was sentenced to 12 years in prison.

"There are a lot of bleeding hearts around who just don't like to see people with helmets and guns. All I can say is, go on and bleed. . . ."
– Prime Minister Pierre Trudeau after invoking the War Measures Act during the 1970 October Crisis.

2000: On September 13, the day after publishing a front page story on the biker war, veteran *Journal de Montreal* crime reporter Michel Auger is shot six times in the newspaper's parking lot. He survives.

2001: Police arrest 120 bikers and their associates in Operation Springtime.

2002: Hell's Angels leader Maurice "Mom" Boucher is found guilty of ordering the murders of two prison guards and is sentenced to life in prison.

2006: On September 13, gunman Kimveer Gill kills one student and injures 19 others at Dawson College before turning the gun on himself.

SERVICE DE POLICE DE LA VILLE DE MONTREAL
- In 2005, the Service de Police de la Ville de Montreal employed 4,289 police officers
- The Service de Police de la Ville de Montreal break the city into four operating centres with a total of 39 police stations: North: 12; South: 6; East: 9 and West: 12

Did you know...

that the British Army policed Montreal until the first Montreal police force was created in 1838? Organized like the military, it consisted of 102 privates, four mounted patrols, six sergeants, six corporals and four officers.

CRIME IN MONTREAL:

A total of 135,781 criminal code infractions and misdemeanors were recorded by Montreal police in 2005, up 5 percent from 2004. Since 2000, however that number has gone down by 13.2 percent. Since 1991, when over more than 218,000 crimes were reported, crime in Montreal has gone down by 37.9 percent.

Montreal Mafia

Thanks to the Port of Montreal, with its opportunities for smuggling narcotics, New York City's Bonanno crime family had long coveted a presence in Montreal.

On several occasions, they sent representatives like notorious Carmine Galente north to make sure they were getting their piece of the Montreal crime pie. But after the authorities consistently thwarted them (deporting Galente), New York crime boss Joseph "Joe Bananas" Bonanno aligned his family with the local Italian mob controlled by Vic "the Egg" Cotroni.

A former professional wrestler (using the name Vic Vincent), Cotroni and his associates, including his brothers Frank and Giusepe, right-hand man (and fellow Calabrian) Paolo Violi and Nicolo "Nick" Rizzuto, controlled the Montreal underworld, running drugs, gambling rings, prostitutes and other rackets. It is estimated that by the 1960s two-thirds of the heroin in North America was entering through Montreal.

By the mid-1970s, however, war broke out inside the Cotroni family after the Godfather named Paolo Violi his successor. By 1981, the war between the Cotronis and Rizzutos took some 20 lives, including Paolo Violi's. Eventually Nick Rizzuto and his son Vito emerged as winners and took over control of the Montreal Mafia.

Rizzuto patriarch Nick is alive and well at age 83, but has been in prison since November 2006 awaiting trial on charges he was part of a group bringing cocaine through Montreal's Trudeau airport. Rizzuto's son Vito, the alleged Godfather of the Montreal Mafia today, was extradited to the United States in August 2006, and has since pled guilty to racketeering charges: He received a 10-year sentence in May 2007. He is 61.

CRIMES AGAINST PROPERTY (2005):

- Cases of arson: 769
- Break-ins: 19,533
- Motor vehicle thefts: 14,129
- Thefts: 44,253
- Cases of Fraud: 5,532

Biker Wars

In the 1980s, some Canadian motorcycle gangs made the leap from being petty criminals to serious players in the lucrative illegal drug trade. For many years, Montrealers tended to tolerate their activities, because the victims usually were other criminals or rival bike gangs.

Quebec biker wars escalated in 1994 when a new gang, the Rock Machine, tried to move in on the Hell's Angels' drug turf. Over the next several years, the war between the two gangs and their associates would claim over 150 lives.

Public outcry followed when a car bomb exploded on a Montreal street on August 9, 1995, killing 11-year-old Daniel Desrochers. A month later, the Wolverine Task Force composed of elite RCMP, Sûrété du Québec and MUC Police officers, was formed with the explicit mandate to investigate biker crime.

Bikers responded with more violence. In 1997, Hell's hitmen shot and killed two Quebec prison guards. The day after his front page story on biker gangs was published, veteran Journal de Montreal crime reporter Michel Auger was shot six times in the newspaper parking lot. The violence finally abated after March 2001, when police nabbed some 120 bikers and their associates in a series of coordinated raids known as Operation Springtime. The trials that ensued saw dozens of bikers given lengthy prison sentences.

CRIMES AGAINST PERSONS:
- Homicides: 35
- Attempted murder: 141
- Sexual assaults: 1,750
- Robberies and extortions: 4,340
- Assaults: 14,027

Of the 34,844 criminal charges laid in Montreal in 2005, 3,323 were against juveniles, including six homicide and four attempted murder charges.

ALARM BELLS

In 2005, the Montreal police's alarm management system handled over 43,000 alarm calls, 40,493 of which were false alarms. Of the 2,872 real alarms, 2,398 were for break-ins and 474 were for hold-ups. The police estimate the cost of answering the false alarms to be over $2 million.

- Montreal police officers fired their guns 40 times in 10 different incidents in 2005. In one incident, a shootout with an armed suspect, 30 shots were fired. Four others gunshots were fired accidentally.
- Montreal police officers used pepper spray 120 times in 2005, down from 213 in 2000.

Did you know...

that when the Canadian loonie was initially introduced, a third of the 15,000 parking meters in the city of Montreal were unable to distinguish between a loonie and a household washer? The cost for a roll of 80 washers at a hardware store was about five dollars.

MONTREAL POLICE OFFICERS THAT HAVE DIED IN THE LINE OF DUTY

- Constable Robert Baril, 42 – Shot, 1986
- Constable John Beatty, 22 – Beaten, 1885
- Constable Paul Beaucage, 28 – Stabbed, 1931
- Constable Jean B. Beaudry, 30 – Shot, 1923
- Patrolman Pierre Beaulieu, 38 – Shot, 1984
- Detective Sergeant Gilles Beauvais, 37 – 1975 (circumstances unavailable)
- Constable Honore Bourdon, 36 – Beaten, 1914
- Constable Lucien Bourgela, 42 – 1939 (circumstances unclear)
- Constable Gilles Boutin, 29 – 1969 (circumstances unavailable)
- Constable Pierre Brule, 31 – Struck by a car, 1981
- Constable Bernard Charlebois, 27 – 1971 (circumstances unclear)
- Constable Thomas Chicoine, 31 – 1920 (circumstances unclear)
- Constable Emmanuel Cloutier, 51 – Shot, 1981
- Constable Paul E. Duranleau, 34 – 1948 (circumstances unclear)
- Constable Henri Farmer, 34 – Shot, 1944
- Constable Jules Fortin, 33 – Shot, 1910
- Constable Jacinthe Fyfe, 25 – Shot, 1985
- Constable Charles Houle, 32 – 1957 (circumstances unavailable)
- Detective Sergeant Gilles Jean, 35 – 1968 (circumstances unavailable)
- Constable Marcel Lacombe, 45 – 1961 (circumstances unavailable)
- Constable Serge Laforest, 35 – 1982 (circumstances unavailable)
- Constable André Lalonde, 51 – Shot, 1996
- Constable Richard Larente, 26 – Shot, 1973
- Detective Sergeant Robert Larue, 50 – Shot, 1984
- Corrections Officer Diane Lavigne, age unknown – Shot, 1997
- Constable Benoit L'Écuyer, 29 – Shot, 2002
- Constable John Malone, 26 – Beaten, 1885
- Constable Alain Matte, 37 – Motor vehicle collision, 2000
- Constable Daniel O'Connell, 35 – Shot, 1910
- Constable Nelson Paquin, 41 – 1948 (circumstances unclear)

- Constable Aimé Pelletier, 39 – 1974 (circumstances unavailable)
- Constable Dollard Pelletier, 44 – Shot, 1930
- Constable Yves Phaneuf, 25 – Shot, 1991
- Constable Odette Pinard, 30 – Shot, 1995
- Corrections Officer Pierre Rondeau, 49 – Shot, 1997
- Constable Jean G. Sabourin, 36 – 1971 (circumstances unavailable)
- Constable Georges Shea, 26 – Shot, 1908
- Constable Claude St. Laurent, 33 – Shot, 1986
- Constable René Vallée, 28 – Shot, 1979
- Constable Léo Villeneuve, 31 – 1928 (circumstances unclear)

Source: Canadian Police and Peace Officers.

Maurice "Mom" Boucher

Born in 1953 in the Hochelaga-Maisoneuve district in Montreal's east end, Maurice Boucher had a criminal record by the age of 19 and had served his first prison sentence (40 months for armed robbery) in 1976. In 1987, Boucher joined the Montreal Chapter of the Hell's Angels, rising quickly through the ranks to become president of the Montreal chapter and one of the most powerful criminals in Quebec.

In December 1997, Boucher was charged with the murder Diane Lavigne, one of two Quebec prison guards murdered in drive-by shootings that year. The prosecution's star witness was Stephane "Godasse" Gagne, a member of the Hell's puppet club, the Rockers MC, who admitted being the triggerman in the Lavigne murder. Gagne claimed that Boucher had ordered the murders.

Boucher was acquitted, but the prosecution appealed, citing jury tampering, and the verdict was thrown out. On October 2000, Boucher was arrested again (he awaited trial in solitary confinement in his own wing of a prison for women), this time facing 13 more murder charges. In April 2002, 49-year-old Maurice "Mom" Boucher was found guilty of ordering the murders of the prison guards and sentenced to life in prison with no possibility of parole for 25 years. He is serving his sentence in Canada's only super-maximum security prison in Ste.-Anne-des-Plaines, Quebec.

TRAFFIC VIOLATIONS
- Total number of moving violations issued: 275,898
- Total number of speeding tickets issued: 143,657
- Total number of parking infractions: 122,893
- Total number of traffic summonses: 542,448

Source: Service de police de la Ville de Montréal.

POLICING MONTREAL
- In 2006, there were 821 citizens (in GMA) per one Montreal Police department officer (compared to 523 officers per 100,000 population in Toronto)
- In 2006 there were 5,768 people working for the MPS, 4,383 of whom were police officers while the remaining 1,385 were civilians. Of the 4,383 officers on the job 3,128 or 71.3 percent of them were men; the remaining 1,255 or 28.7 percent were women.
- The total number of staff with the MPS (2006): 5,768 (4,383 police officers, 1,385 civilians)
- The average wait time for priority calls to MPS: 5.9 minutes in 2006, down from 6.4 minutes in 2005
- There are 49 Neighbourhood Police Stations (NPS) in Montreal, each operating under one of four Community Service Stations.
- The MPS boasts three electric cars, 438 cars (marked), 79 mini-vans (marked), 515 other vehicles (unmarked and semi-unmarked), 4 all terrain vehicles, 42 motorcycles, 113 parking enforcement vehicles, 35 trucks, and 6 boats.

They Said It

"What is the Mafia? I made my money in clubs and gambling. All the rest is nothing but talk."
– Montreal Godfather Vincenzo "Vic the Egg" Cotroni.

Take 5 FIVE MONTREAL BAD GUY NICKNAMES

1. **Denis "Pas Fiable" Houle** (Unreliable)
2. **Vincenzo "Vic the Egg" Cotroni**
3. **Allan "the Weasel" Ross**
4. **Jean-Pierre "Matt Le Crosseur" Mathieu** (Matt the Backstabber)
5. **Maurice "Mom" Boucher** (his nickname isn't some evil acronym. He allegedly earned it because he liked to cook breakfast for his fellow Hell's Angels.)

Source: Montreal Crime Web Pages.

BROTHER ANDRE'S HEART

A porter and religious brother at Montreal's College Notre-Dame, Brother Andre (born Alfred Bessette) went on to become one of the most important Roman Catholic figures in Canada. A humble orphan, Brother Andre is credited with helping as many as 15,000 crippled, blind and dying pilgrims a year by praying to St. Joseph, his patron saint. When he died in 1937, half million people walked past his casket.

In death, Brother Andre's heart was preserved in an urn, serving as a beacon for pilgrims from around the world. In one of the most bizarre crimes in Canadian history, thieves broke into the Oratory and stole Brother Andre's heart on March 15, 1973. The burglary was the work of professionals, who had to pick three locks and chisel the urn off its pedestal, all without alerting the security guards who regularly patrolled the oratory.

Eventually the heart was discovered in the basement of a home on Montreal's South Shore. It was put back on display with the addition of a security system so that it could continue to serve as an object of contemplation for pilgrims.

SALARY

The Montreal Police department pay scale is competitive with other Canadian police services. The following is a breakdown of the salary range for the rank of constable. A constable's pay class increases on their anniversary date during the first six years of service.

Class Annually 2007 ($/year)
- 6th Class Constable $39,280
- 5th Class Constable $43,941
- 4th Class Constable $49,267
- 3rd Class Constable $55,253
- 2nd Class Constable $59,919
- 1st Class Constable $66,577

Source: Service de police de la Ville de Montréal.

CAR THEFT

Montreal was long known as the car theft capital of Canada, but that distinction is now held by the city of Winnipeg. With 14,129 cars stolen in 2005, Montreal ranked fourth in Canada for the rate of car thefts in major metropolitan centres, with a rate of 649 per 100,000. Winnipeg had a car theft rate of 1,712 followed by Edmonton at 1,059 and Vancouver at 990. Montreal's recovery rate for stolen cars is thought to be among the lowest of all Canadian cities, with many of the vehicles quickly disappearing into shipping containers at the Port of Montreal.

Sources: Service de Police de la Ville de Montreal; Statistics Canada.

Did you know...

that convicted schoolgirl killer Karla Homolka lives in the Montreal area? She settled in the city after completing her sentence in a Quebec prison in 2005.

Weblinks

Service de Police de la Ville de Montreal

www.spvm.qc.ca/en/index.asp

Start here if you want to do some sleuthing around Montreal's police force. Find services for the public, neighbourhood police, publications and information. Want to become an officer? Here's what to do. The site also features profiles of Montreal's missing persons and most wanted.

Sûrété du Québec

www.surete.qc.ca/

A site dedicated to the provincial police service that will keep you updated on police-related news, publications, recruitment and more.

Montreal Police Convicted

www.thecanadianencyclopedia.com/index.cfm?PgNm=TCE&Params=M1ARTM0010446

Read *Maclean's* story from 1995 in which four members of the service de Police de la Ville de Montreal were convicted of assault. That case shed light on a number of other related cases.

Culture

Culture is not an embellishment in Montreal — it's an industry. As the only French-speaking metropolis in the Americas, it has created its own parallel universe of stars (vedettes in French) who are often unknown anywhere else in North America, although many of them like singer Roch Voisine and actress Marie-Josée Croze have large European followings.

Movies by such local luminaries as Denys Arcand, Louis Bélanger and Jean-François Pouliot routinely outdraw Hollywood blockbusters. Plays by Robert Lepage and Michel Tremblay fill local theatres and the antics of rock bands like Les Cowboys Fringants (the Frisky Cowboys) and Les Colocs fill the pages of local fanzines. The French television networks create their own dramas, talk shows and soap operas (or télé-romans).

But the city has also been a fertile ground for anglophone artists, performers and writers as well — people like novelists Hugh Maclennan and Mordecai Richler, poets Irving Layton and Leonard Cohen, actors William Shatner, Neil Bissoondath and Christopher Plummer, rock bands like Arcade Fire, singers like Rufus Wainwright and the McGarrigle Sisters, and jazz musicians like Oscar Peterson.

Montreal's easy, laid back attitude tempts a fair number of anglophone artists and performers from abroad to make the city their home

> "I mean, the way I see it is, every penny I've ever made through music is free money."
>
> **– Rock bassist Melissa auf der Maur**

at least temporarily. Irish novelist Brian Moore did some of his most productive work in Montreal and set several of his stories in the city. Some, like musicians Jesse Winchester and Charlie Biddle, settled in Montreal permanently.

ARTISTS

Montreal ranks second after Toronto for the number of artists and is third after Vancouver and Victoria in per capita artistic concentration. The city doesn't pay its artists particularly well compared with other cities, but their income is closer to the city's overall average than in any other city.

- Number of artists in Canada: 130,700 (0.8 per cent of the workforce)
- Number in Montreal: 10,075 (1.9 per cent of the workforce)
- Montreal artists' average earnings: $26,245
- Gap between artists' earnings and overall workforce average: 7 per cent

MONTREAL HAS

- 1,530 producers, directors and choreographers
- 1,325 actors
- 1,225 musicians and singers
- 1,195 writers
- 770 painters and sculptors
- 695 artisans
- 270 dancers

Did you know...

> that one of Montreal's prolific writers of "tele-romans" was Lise Payette, better known outside Quebec as a minister in the Parti Québécois government of René Lévesque from 1976-81?

ALL IN A YEAR'S WORK

- Writers $30,503
- Producers, directors and choreographers $29,135
- Actors $24,074
- Artisans $19,104
- Painters and sculptors $18,484
- Dancers $18,299
- Musicians and singers $15,676

Source: Canadian Council for the Arts.

An Ancient Art for The Modern World

The two biggest draws in Las Vegas these days — after the slots, of course — are both Montreal products: Céline Dion and the Cirque du Soleil. In fact, the Cirque has two venues in the American gambling capital and another at Walt Disney World, as well as several touring companies making the round of major cities in Asia and Europe.

Sadly, this global phenomenon has no permanent venue in Montreal, but its head office (with 1,600 employees) is still in the city and one of its touring companies does pitch its distinctive blue-and-yellow tents on the waterfront every couple of years or so.

The Cirques founders were a troupe of street performers from the little village of Baie St-Paul led by Guy Laliberté and Gilles Ste-Croix. In 1984, Laliberté persuaded the organizers of the celebrations marking the 450th anniversary of Jacques Cartier's voyage to Canada to let him stage a show he called the Cirque du Soleil.

What he came up with was a brilliant reworking of the ancient circus theme that blended music, dance, and breathtaking acrobatics. To guarantee success he added a dash of earthy humour and some daringly erotic costumes. The result was a smashing success, and now close to 60 million people around the world have seen a live Cirque show.

PLATEAU

Montreal's Plateau neighbourhood area has the highest concentration of artists in the country, according to an examination of neighbourhoods by Hill Strategies.

ARTS ORGANIZED

Montreal's Conseil des arts has been around since 1956, which makes it Canada's first municipal arts council. Its grants in 2007 totaled nearly $8.4 million shared among 274 non-profit artistic groups and associations. Musical and theatre programs got more than half the money with 62 musical groups sharing $2.2 million and 55 theatre groups sharing $2.5 million. Visual arts, media arts, dance, cinema and new arts shared the rest. The council also provides rehearsal space for performing artists and serves as a liaison between the artistic community and the city.

CULTURAL SPENDING

Despite the high concentration of artists and performers, Montrealers are not big spenders when it comes to the arts. Their annual per-capita spending ($750) ranks 12th of 15 Canadian metropolitan areas. Of the $2.6 billion Montrealers spent on culture:
- $1.3 billion (49 percent) on home entertainment
- $570 million (22 percent) on reading materials
- $220 million (9 percent) on photographic equipment
- $210 million (8 percent) on arts events, works and live performing arts
- $170 million (7 percent) on movies
- $120 million (5 percent) on art supplies

Source: Statistics Canada.

Did you know...

that the Suzanne of poet-songwriter Leonard Cohen's most famous love ode was dancer Suzanne Verdal who now lives in Venice Beach, California, in a homemade camper on the back of a truck?

ALL IN ORDER
- Montrealers who are recipients of the Order of Canada: 505
- Officers of the Order of Canada: 16
- Members of the Order of Canada: 434
- Companions of the Order: 55

Bio MORDECAI RICHLER

Mordecai Richler created some of the most memorable characters in Canadian fiction from the irrepressible and less-than-entirely-honest Duddy Kravitz to Jacob Two Two, pint-sized conqueror of dinosaurs and hooded fangs. But Richler's greatest creation was probably himself —the irascible, disheveled outsider who dared to mutter, drink in hand, what no one else dared to say.

If his fiction entertained, his essays and magazine articles on life in Quebec could infuriate. His lampooning of Quebec's nationalism and intrusive language laws prompted one exasperated critic to sputter that Richler wasn't a "real Quebecer."

Cutting words, indeed, for a man who was born and brought up in the Jewish ghetto around rue St-Urbain right in the heart of Montreal. He might never have learned to speak French properly, but Richler was pure Montreal. He lived in Europe from 1959-'71 but wrote at the time: "No matter how long I live abroad, I do feel forever rooted in St. Urbain Street. That was my time, my place, and I have elected myself to get it right."

And get it right he did, in a whole series of novels that described with wit and colour life in the Jewish quarter of Mile End. It was a hardscrabble place to grow up. Born the son of a scrap-yard dealer in 1931, Richler never had much money. He graduated from Baron Byng High School, an academy he immortalized in St. Urbain's Horseman, but never finished his English degree at Sir George Williams University. Now literature students at his old school — since renamed Concordia — study his books.

FILM

Montrealers love movies, and what they love most are movies about themselves. With a captive audience like that, it's no wonder that Montreal studios are so prolific. In the rest of Canada, going to see a made-in-Canada flick might often be seen as a cultural duty; in Montreal, it's just pure entertainment.

Take 5 BRYAN DEMCHINSKY'S TOP FIVE LITERARY SPOTS

Bryan Demchinsky was the literary editor of the *Montreal Gazette* for eleven years. He is the author, with Elaine Kalman Naves, of *Storied Streets: Montreal in the Literary Imagination* and he has written and edited several other books on the subject of Montreal's history and architecture. Montreal, he says, has been created by its writers as much as its builders. Among the locales that are intimately associated with the city are:

1. **Mount Royal.** The mountain defines Montreal as a place and an act of the imagination. Jacques Cartier climbed its flank in 1535 and returned to France with the wondrous tale of a native village called Hochelaga. Nearly every writer that the city has seen has been inspired by the mountain. A.M. Klein, Yves Thériault, Irving Layton, Monique Proulx, Jacques Godbout and many others have climbed to the summit that Cartier named.

2. **Place d'Armes.** History is embodied in the square around which stands the architecture of the city's different eras. Visiting 19th-century writers like Henri David Thoreau and Washington Irving marveled at the towering basilica of Notre Dame, while in more recent times Hubert Aquin, Hugh MacLennan and Ringuet have visited it or its Old Montreal environs.

QUEBEC STARS

The nascent Quebec industry took a heavy hit in the 1950s when television largely emptied local theatres. But in the 1960s, the federally funded National Film Board breathed new life into Quebec films by producing a number of popular documentaries and full-length features including Claude Jutra's *Mon Oncle Antoine* (1971). The film industry really came of age in the 1980s and '90s with directors like Jean-Claude Lauzon (*Un zoo la nuit*, 1987), Léa Pool (*Le Papillon bleu*, 2004) and Charles Binamé (*Un homme et son péché*, 2002).

3. **Place Portugal.** The little park at the corner of St-Laurent Boulevard and Marie-Anne Street is a tranquil oasis on the edge of the bustling Main. It's an ideal spot to contemplate Montreal's literary diversity. To the east is the teeming Plateau of Michel Tremblay and Yves Beauchemin. To the west is Mordecai Richler's St-Urbain Street. And as the park's name suggests, waves of immigrants still arrive to refresh the city's roots. As a bonus, a house owned by Leonard Cohen stands on one corner of the square.

4. **Peel and Ste-Catherine.** A river of commerce flows through the heart of Montreal, and its epicentre is Peel and Ste-Catherine. Mordecai Richler, Gabrielle Roy, poet Jean Narrache and Hugh MacLennan are among many writers who have celebrated Ste-Catherine's energy.

5. **St. Louis Square**. In 1898, Emile Nelligan, the young poet laureate who symbolized Quebec's literary coming of age, climbed a tree in St-Louis Square and refused to come down, signalling that the madness that attended his genius had taken control of him. He never wrote another poem, but the square has remained a fixture in Montreal's literature. Fittingly, the Union des Écrivains has its headquarters there.

By far the best-known of this crop of auteurs is Denys Arcand, who originally dreamed of being a professional tennis player. When Arcand's *Invasions Barbares* (Barbarian Invasions) won the Academy Award for best foreign-language film in 2003, it simply confirmed for the world what Quebecers had long known - that films about life in Quebec can be every bit as satisfying as blockbusters about superheroes. And it's not just the quality of the films that impressive, but their range as well. They include bittersweet romance like *Gaz Bar Blues*, vitriolic nationalist screed like *Octobre*, whimsical comedies like *La Grande Séduction*, and true-life gangster flicks like *Monica la mitraille* (Machine Gun Molly).

Take 5 FIVE ENGLISH LANGUAGE MOVIES STARRING MONTREAL AS SOMEWHERE ELSE

1. *Pluto Nash* with Eddie Murphy
2. *The Art of War* with Wesley Snipes
3. *The Bone Collector* with Denzel Washington
4. *Once Upon a Time In America* with Robert de Niro
5. *The Sum of All Fears* with Ben Affleck

Bio CÉLINE DION

Love her or hate her — and there are plenty on both sides of that ledger — you can't escape the formidable Céline Dion. She has sold more than 100 million albums worldwide, and her soaring voice booms out of tape decks and CD players from Vegas to Venice.

Technically, Céline's not really a Montrealer. The youngest of 14 children, she was born in 1968 in Charlemagne just off Montreal Island. Her devoutly Catholic parents ran a little piano bar where she and her siblings entertained the patrons. But even by age 12, Céline was hungering for something a little more than a honky-tonk in the burbs. So her family shipped a demo she'd recorded to promoter René Angelil. The story goes that he was so moved he mortgaged his house to produce the album that rocketed Céline to the top of the Quebec pop scene.

Convinced he had more than a small-market star on his hands, Angelil had Céline cut her hair, cap her teeth and learn English, the official language of stardom. It paid off. In 1990 she hit it big in the United States with *Unison* and has seldom put a foot wrong since. Everything Céline touches seems to turn into a gold.

Despite her success and her two Oscars and five Grammys, Céline has a hard time getting any respect from her critics who rag her endlessly for her accent, her clothes and her shamelessly sentimental lyrics. Her marriage in 1990 to Angelil, 26 years her senior and the veteran of two earlier marriages, didn't help her image much, either.

There's a whiff of envy in all the carping. Céline has earned her success with a powerful voice, a prodigious appetite for hard work, and an unerring instinct for what her fans want. And critics or no critics, she still packs 4,000 fans into Caesar's Palace four nights a week to watch her perform.

JOHN AND YOKO

John Lennon and Yoko Ono held their legendary Bed-In from May 26 to June 2nd, 1969 in Suite 1742 at the Fairmont's Queen Elizabeth hotel in downtown Montreal. There, surrounded by celebrities such as Tommy Smothers, Timothy and Rosemary Leary and Petula Clark, they wrote the peace anthem, "Give Peace a Chance."

Take 5 FIVE MOVIES ABOUT MONTREAL:

1. *The Luck of Ginger Coffey* (1964). Robert Shaw and Mary Ure star in a Brian Moore heartbreaker about an Irish immigrant trying to become a journalist and hold his marriage together.
2. *The Apprenticeship of Duddy Kravitz* (1974). Richard Dreyfuss plays a young Jewish entrepreneur on the make in a richly atmospheric recreation of Mordecai Richler's novel.
3. *Jésus de Montréal* (1989). An all Quebec cast stars in Denys Arcand's mystical film about a porn actor hired to play the part of Jesus in an open-air mystery play.
4. *Les Invasions Barabares* (2003): Director Denys Arcand won the Academy Award for best foreign-language film with this brilliant tragi-comic tale of love, death and disillusion.
5. *Bon Cop Bad Cop* (2006). A gangland slaying right on the Quebec-Ontario border provides a vehicle for some bilingual laughs as a detective from the Sûreté du Québec and one from the Ontario Provincial Police try to co-operate to solve the case.

NOT ALWAYS HARMONIOUS

The Montreal Symphony Orchestra has a well-deserved world reputation for excellence, if not always for harmony. It has had a succession of colourful conductors since it was founded in 1934, starting with Sir Wilfrid Pelletier and including such well-known musicians as Franz-Paul Decker and Zubin Mehta (under whom it became the first Canadian orchestra to tour Europe).

But the man who cemented its reputation as a world-class group was Swiss-born Charles Dutoit, who wielded the baton from 1977 to

Indie Paradise

Montreal has everything a starving wannabe rock star could want: cheap rents, plenty of homegrown recording labels, a high percentage of college and university students and lots of abandoned industrial buildings to practice in.

And live music is very much in with such venues as the Casa del Popolo, the Sala Rosa and the impossibly cramped but very hip Barfly leading the way. In fact, Montreal's indie scene is so lively that in 2006, publications as diverse as *Spin* and the *New York Times* started referring to the city as the next Seattle.

Arcade Fire, of course, which has taken the world by storm since it burst onto the scene in 2005, is the most successful and best-known product of the indie subculture, but it has plenty of bands breathing down its neck — the Dears, Wolf Parade, The Stills and, of course, the pioneering Godspeed You Black Emperor, which blazed the trail for everyone else back in the 1990s when it opened the Hotel2Tango as a live venue.

But the interesting thing about Montreal is that there is a whole parallel universe of francophone bands that sell thousands of CDs to their home-province fans and tour Europe but that are barely known in the rest of North America (the Cowboys Fringants and Mes Aïeux are two examples).

2002. The symphony became particularly noted for its daring interpretation of the works of Maurice Ravel. Dutoit was also quick to jump on the classical recording bandwagon. The MSO is as well known for its records and CDs as it is for its concerts.

Take 5 — FILMMAKER LEWIS COHEN'S FIVE FAVOURITE OUTDOOR SHOOTING LOCATIONS

Montreal filmmaker Lewis Cohen has filmed in cities from Frankfurt to Vegas, but his preferred locations have always been in his hometown. Cohen has authored hours of acclaimed television programs, including the prime-time Emmy Award winning television series *Cirque du Soleil: Fire Within*.

1. **Mount Royal:** Go to the lookout on the eastern slope, with a view of the Olympic Stadium. Walk up the staircase at the upper edge of the parking lot and hold to the path on your left for at least 250 meters. This partially hidden corridor offers many spectacular views of the city, some seen through a light blush of foliage. As you walk the path, downtown is slowly revealed, like a long dolly shot naturally unfolding. Stunning in all seasons — it's a visual wonder to see the city lit up through snow covered branches or, like in Denys Arcand's *Jesus of Montreal*, through the thick greenery of summer. Best at sunrise or sunset.

2. **Rue St. Dizier:** This tiny one block cobblestone alleyway off the rue de la Commune in Old Montreal has a moody, Kafkaesque quality after the sunsets. Tall, old and narrow, it's a perfect location for a mysterious rainy or snowy night shoot. Equally important, it borders on some of the loveliest buildings in the old city, and is across the street from the waterfront park at the edge of the St. Lawrence River.

3. **Around Wilensky's:** A vintage 1950's diner with old wooden stools set atop a black and white tiled floor, Wilensky's is located at Fairmount and Clark in the heart of the Mile End. The storefront and interior hasn't changed a whit since the 1950s when Mordecai Richler used it as a setting in his early novels. The alleyways of this neighbour-

NOTABLE WRITING

Until well into the 20th century, Montreal writers pretty much ignored urban life and, instead, romanticized the simple lives of the rural habitants or extolled the past glories of Nouvelle France. Industrialization, a couple of world wars and the Depression changed all that, and life in

hood are equally visual, mixing tenement-style back porches, with innovative new design and an occasional old horse stable. You'll recognize these lanes from *Lies My Father Told Me*, and countless other Montreal movies. Bonus: Fairmount Bagel's wood ovens are a few steps away, and open 24 hours.

4. **The Geodesic Dome:** Buckminster Fuller and Shoji Sadao designed this lightly filigreed twenty-story high sphere to be the US pavilion at Expo 67. Just before the break of day about ten years ago, I filmed two California-based performance artists scaling this massive structure in one of their architectural 'interventions'. The subtle, transparent skin that divides inside from outside makes this surreal sphere a fascinating place to shoot or just to walk around—could be home to a great action sequence, a thoughtful protagonist or a Bjork music video. Redubbed the Biosphere, and located atop the St. Lawrence River, this unique structure now contains an interactive museum designed to raise awareness of the environment.

5. **Cité du cirque:** Over the past two decades the Cirque du Soleil has transformed an old garbage dump in an underdeveloped corner of northeast Montreal into a state of the art circus complex; including studios, workshops, a circus school and a theatre. This sprawling complex near the corner of Jarry and Iberville is less of an architectural wonder and more of a voyeuristic opportunity to glimpse the place where the world's most successful creator of live entertainment has its factory-like headquarters. I spent many days and evenings outside the buildings to capture an atmospheric peek through the aluminum curtains. As show deadlines approach, costume designers work late into the night, acrobats fly and artists shuttle back and forth between rehearsals and their Japanese-style dormitory across the street from the training center.

1. **Céline Dion** (pop diva)
2. **Oscar Peterson** (musician)
3. **William Shatner** (actor)
4. **Leonard Cohen** (poet and songwriter)
5. **Christopher Plummer** (actor)

the big city became the dominant theme in the works of local writers.

The Révolution tranquille of the 1960s and '70s ushered in something of a golden age of Quebec literature with novelists like Claire Blais, Hubert Aquin, Réjean Ducharme, and Jacques Godbout poets like Marcel Dubé and playwrights like Michel Tremblay.

GRAND PRIX

The Grand Prix of Canada, the first Formula 1 race in North America, is held every year in Montreal at the Circuit Gilles-Villeneuve. The second North American Formula 1 race was held in Indianapolis for the first time on September 24th, 2000. The Canadian Grand Prix is the sporting event that generates the most economic spin-offs in Canada. In 2004, 317,000 spectators were in attendance. Since 2001, the Circuit Gilles-Villeneuve has also hosted the Montreal Molson Indy.

Take 5 TOP MONTREAL SPORTS TEAMS

Montreal Canadiens, NHL (24 Championships)
Montreal Alouettes, CFL (7 Championships)
Montreal Impact, USL (2 Championships)
Montreal Expos, MLB – Now the Washington Nationals
(0 Championships)
Montreal Royal, ABA (0 Championships)

Take 5 FIVE GREAT TV SERIES CREATED IN MONTREAL

1. **La Famille Plouffe**
2. **Les Belles histoires des Pays-d'en-Haut**
3. **Les Bourdon**
4. **Des dames de coeur**
5. **Les filles de Caleb**

THE REAL HOCKEYTOWN

On March 3rd, 1875, the very first hockey game in the world was played at the Victoria rink in Montreal. The game apparently ended in a fight. No city is more closely associated with hockey than Montreal. Today, the game is widely played, not only in arenas, but also on outdoor rinks in city parks and suburban backyards. In the warmer months, a tennis ball substitutes for a puck, and driveways and streets stand in for sheets of ice.

The Montreal Canadiens' 24 championships lead all NHL teams (the Toronto Maple Leafs are a distant second with 13), and the Habs, (short for Habitants) consistently sell out home games at the Bell Centre. A hall of fame could be stocked just with Montreal-born hockey greats – Doug Harvey, Maurice and Henri Richard, Mario Lemieux, Mike Bossy, Raymond Bourque and Martin Brodeur among them. Many other stars including Jacques Plante, Jean Beliveau, Guy Lafleur, Marcel Dionne and Patrick Roy have hailed from elsewhere in Quebec, and countless others born outside the province have found fame playing in Montreal. Habs' coaches have included such legends as Dick Irvin Sr., Toe Blake and Scotty Bowman.

They Said It

> "Coming from Canada, being a writer and Jewish as well, I have impeccable paranoia credentials."
>
> **– Mordecai Richler**

A MONTREAL HOCKEY CHRONOLOGY:

1875: Hockey, in roughly its current form, is played for the first time at Victoria Skating Rink on Drummond Street in Montreal.

1893: The Montreal Amateur Athletic Association hockey club is awarded the first Stanley Cup.

1909: The Montreal Canadiens are established as a Francophone response to the Anglo supported Montreal Wanderers.

1916: The Canadiens, led by goaltender George Vézina and player-coach Newsy Lalonde, win their first Stanley Cup.

1917: The National Hockey League (NHL) is founded at a meeting at Montreal's Windsor Hotel; the five original members are the Canadiens, the Montreal Wanderers, the Ottawa Senators, the Quebec Bulldogs and the Toronto Arenas.

1918: The Montreal arena on Ste. Catherine Street in Westmount, home to the Montreal Wanderers and Montreal Canadiens, burns down. The Canadiens relocate, but the Wanderers fold.

1918: Montreal Canadiens' goaltender Georges Vézina (the Chicoutimi Cucumber) records the first shutout in NHL history.

1919: Flu epidemic forces cancellation of the last game of the 1919 Stanley Cup finals between the Canadiens and the Seattle Metropolitans. No cup winner is declared.

1924: The Montreal Maroons enter the NHL and play at the newly opened $15 million Montreal Forum.

1937: Canadiens' star Howie Morenz dies suddenly in hospital at age 34. His funeral is held inside a packed Montreal Forum while 15,000 mourners wait outside.

1939: Montreal Maroons fold.

1945: Maurice "Rocket" Richard scores 50 goals in 50 games.

Did you know...

that Saul Bellow, winner of the 1976 Nobel Prize for Literature, was born Solomon Bellow in the Montreal suburb of Lachine in 1915?

1955: Richard is suspended for the playoffs for punching a linesman during a fight at the end of the regular season. The suspension touches off a riot in the Forum and surrounding area.

1960: Les Canadiens, led by Jean Beliveau, Henri Richard, Bernie Geoffrion and Jacques Plante, win their fifth straight Stanley Cup. Maurice Richard retires.

1969: The Canadiens win their fourth Stanley Cup in five years.

1971: Rookie goaltender Ken Dryden, with only 6 games of regular season experience under his belt, backstops the Habs to a Cup win. Jean Beliveau retires in the spring and Guy Lafleur debuts in the fall.

1972: The USSR squad shocks Team Canada with a 7-3 victory on Forum ice in the opening game of the Summit Series.

1975: New Year's Eve game at the Forum pitting the Canadiens against the Soviet Red Army team is considered one of the greatest games ever played and ends in a 3-3 tie.

1979: Les Canadiens starring Lafleur, Shutt, Lemaire, Cournoyer, Gainey, Savard, Lapointe, Robinson and Dryden, and coached by Scotty Bowman, win their fourth straight Stanley Cup.

1986: Rookie goaltender Patrick Roy leads the Canadiens to the Stanley Cup.

1993: The Canadiens win their 24th and most recent Stanley Cup. The current drought represents the longest in franchise history.

1996: Montreal Forum closes; the Canadiens begin play at the Molson Centre, now known as the Bell Centre.

2001: Molson's sells the Canadiens to American George Gillett.

Did you know...

that Expo 67 attracted 50 million visitors during its six month run? Among the more recognizable surviving structures are the avante garde housing complex Habitat 67, the US Pavilion (now the Biosphere) and the French Pavilion (now the Casino de Montreal).

Revolutionary Art

The Musée d'art contemporain is more than just another modern-art museum crammed with abstract paintings and bizarre installations. It's a monument to a seismic shift in Montreal's (and Quebec's) cultural, political and even religious mores.

The museum houses the work of the so-called Automatistes, a group of painters and sculptors who set out in the 1940s to challenge the reigning orthodoxies of the day. They were the precursors of the Révolution tranquille and laid the foundations of the anti-clerical, profoundly secular orthodoxies of modern Quebec.

The group's leader and founder was painter Paul-Émile Borduas (1905-60) who rebelled against the strictly classical rules he'd been taught at Montreal's École des Beaux-Arts and, instead, began splashing his paint onto canvas in a kind of visual version of stream-of-consciousness writing.

He caused a minor sensation when he exhibited 42 of these works in the Théâtre Ermitage in 1942, and was soon attracting disciples from among all the young rebels in the local art schools, notably Jean-Paul Riopelle (1923-2002), Marcel Barbeau (1925-) and Pierre Gauvreau (1922-). The group also attracted a smattering of writers, poets and playwrights. They were very much the in-crowd of the 1940s — anti-church, anti-classical and anti-establishment.

In 1948, Borduas issued the Refus Global, a sweeping manifesto that rejected traditional values ("To hell with the holy-water-sprinkler and the tuque!"), called for opening Quebec up to the world and championed "resplendent anarchy" as the political philosophy best suited to the group's artistic ideals. But for all its caustic criticism and youthful zeal, the Refus Global was something of a last hurrah for the group. Soon afterward both Borduas and Riopelle, the most important figures in the movement, left for Paris, and the group dispersed.

The influence of the group's individual members, however, is incalculable. Long-lived and prolific, they've had an impact on every facet of Quebec life — cultural, artistic, social, political and religious. Their works are the heart and soul of the Musée d'Art Contemporain's 7,000-piece collection.

ORDER UP!

- Number of licensed restaurants, bars and caterers in Montreal: 6,516
- Restaurants per km^2: 64.9
- Different types of national and regional cuisines to choose from: 80
- Rank out of 70 cities worldwide for the cost of a meal: 43

OH, WHAT A NIGHT

- Number of bars in Montreal's tourist districts: 248
- Bars per km^2: 9.5
- Percentage of foreign tourists who go to a bar when they visit the city: 35.3
- Number of 70's-era nightclubs: 3
- Montreal's rank of the overall top ten nightlife capitals worldwide: 5

Source: Tourism Montreal

BICULTURAL NIGHTS

Nightlife in Montreal comes in two flavours — francophone and anglophone — and three shifts: happy hour (cinq-à-sept in French), evening (which runs until 3 a.m.) and after hours (which runs until the revelers fall asleep or the cops show up). It's important to note, however, that these aren't rigid categories. The happy-hour crowd often hangs in until last call and francophones and anglophones mingle easily on each other's turf.

The centre of gravity for anglophone carousers is the three-block stretch of Crescent St. between René Lévesque Blvd. and Sherbrooke St. Crescent's 19th-century bourgeois townhouses and apartment buildings. It has been converted into an almost solid phalanx of bars, restaurants, discos, dance clubs and (for shoppers) boutiques. The

Did you know...

that North America's only Yiddish theatre company stages plays every fall in the Saidye Bronfman Centre?

1. **International Jazz Festival**, the world's largest.
2. **Just For Laughs**, North America's premier comedy festival.
3. **FrancoFolies** brings the best singers from the francophone world to Montreal.
4. **International des Feux Loto-Québec** hosts national fireworks teams from around the world.
5. **Festival des Films du Monde de Montréal** focuses more on indie films rather than Hollywood blockbusters.

action is particularly intense on the block between Ste. Catherine St. and de Maisonneuve Blvd., where it's difficult to find a seat on any of the two dozen outdoor terraces any time after noon during summer.

Nightclub historians should pay a visit to the Sir Winston Churchill, the pub-disco-restaurant that started the Crescent St. craze in the 1960s. A newer landmark is Newtown's, a flashy bar-resto-disco opened by former Formula 1 racer Jacques Villeneuve (the bar's name is a cheeky English translation of the owner's name). The Crescent St. ambience has spread to several parallel thoroughfares, notably Bishop and de la Montagne Streets.

They Said It

"We were basically one and the same, although Jim was just about perfect, and, of course, I am perfect."
— William Shatner chatting about his alter-ego Captain James Kirk of the Starship Enterprise.

Take 5 **"MEGA-VEDETTES"**

WHO FILL THE PAGES OF MONTREAL'S TABLOIDS AND FANZINES BUT BARELY CREATE A RIPPLE IN THE REST OF CANADA

1. **Roch Voisine** (singer)
2. **Ginette Reno** (singer)
3. **Rémy Girard** (actor)
4. **Patrick Huard** (actor)
5. **Les Cowboys Fringants** (rock band)

FRENCH FUN

As you'd expect, the francophone night scene is larger and more diffuse centring on St. Laurent Blvd. and St. Denis St. and the Plateau Mont-Royal and Mile End areas northeast of downtown. The hippest stretch is a block or so off St. Laurent just north of Sherbrooke St. This is where the movie stars — both Quebec and Hollywood —come out to play at spots like the Globe, the Med and the Buona Notte or to shoot a little pool at Le Swimming. Rock fans head to the Casa del Popolo for vegetarian food and live concerts, while cellphone yuppies cruise for dates at the very chic Upstairs Club. A younger crowd haunts the bars and bistros of the stretch of St. Denis between Ste. Catherine and Sherbrooke Streets.

They Said It

"There are so many parallels between my life and Christ's. He was born in a stable. I was born in a Quebec hospital."
— Local comic Sylvain Larocque

MONTREAL MUNCHIES

No introduction to Montreal would be complete without trying three of its famous foods: bagels, smoked meat and poutine. Bagels are so popular in Montreal that a 2007 CBC poll with over a million votes cast put Montreal bagels on the short list for one of the seven wonders of Canada.

Along with bagels, smoked meat has been popular in Montreal since the early 1800s. Montreal has a sizable Jewish community and the smoked meat sandwich is part of their enduring influence. The smoked meat sandwich has become a symbol of the city's cuisine.

Bio BEN WEIDER

Ben Weider was born in Montreal in 1924. He grew up on Coloniale Avenue in the Plateau district, and left school at age 12 to help the family make ends meet. A dancer, boxer and fitness buff as a youth, Weider also spent three years in the Canadian Army; he says he has never once been a "couch potato."

In the 1930s, Ben's brother Joe started what would become a worldwide fitness, nutrition and bodybuilding empire. Ben joined him in the fledgling enterprise, and the duo would go on to define and popularize bodybuilding, turning what had been a marginal activity into a high profile sport. Among Ben Weider's proudest moments was in 1998 when the International Olympic Committee recognized bodybuilding as a sport. Ben Weider founded the International Federation of Bodybuilders (IFBB) www.ifbb.com in 1946 in Montreal, where it remains headquartered. One of the IFBB's first achievements was staging the Mr. Canada contest at the Monument National Theatre on St. Laurent Boulevard in 1946. Today, the IFBB is active in 176 countries and sponsors numerous strength and bodybuilding events.

Building the perfect body is only one side of Ben Weider. He is also a renowned historian and author. Weider has written books on fitness and nutrition, as well as a biography of Montreal strongman

They Said It

Locals and tourists alike make it a must.

According to montrealpoutine.com, the first poutines were invented in Quebec. "The earliest date associated with its invention is 1957,

Louis Cyr. He may be best known, however, for his decades long work as a Napoleonic scholar. For the last forty-five years, Weider, author of six books on the French General, has sought to demonstrate that contrary to the belief of traditional scholars, Napoleon did not die of cancer, but was in fact poisoned by one his associates.

Ben Weider is founder of the International Napoleonic Society, and one of the world's leading institutions of Napoleon scholarship, Florida State University, established the Weider Eminent Scholar Chair in Napoleonic History in his honor. Florida State has also presented Weider with an Honorary Doctorate of Laws Degree.

Ben Weider is an Officer of the Order of Canada and a Knight of the Order of St. Johns. He is also a recipient Quebec's National Medal as well as that of the French Legion of Honor. Ben and Joe Weider are authors of the book Brothers of Iron: Building the Weider Empire. In addition to his scholarly and business activities, Ben is also an active philanthropist who has donated numerous fitness centres to schools and other institutions in the Montreal area, and around the world. Montreal's Jewish Community Centre in Côte-des-Neiges is named in his honor. Ben Weider is the father of three children and lives in the Hampstead area of Montreal with his wife of 47 years, Huguette.

> *"Poetry is just the evidence of life. If your life is burning well, poetry is just the ash."*
>
> **– Leonard Cohen**

which is when restaurantuer Fernand LaChance of Warwick claims that a take-out customer at his restaurant Lutin Qui Rit, requested french fries, cheese in a bag, to which the restaurateur responded: 'ça va faire une maudite poutine' (That's going to make a damn mess).

In his 2005 obituary, CTV.ca quoted Eddy Lanaisse as that original customer: 'I wanted fries, but I saw cheese curds on the counter. I asked Fernand to mix them together.' LaChance's restaurant eventually closed, and so there exists no present day monument to this earliest claim. Adding gravy to the cheese and fries came sometime later. You can also get it with smoked meat spaghetti sauce.

JAZZ PRETENDER OR …

Despite the fact that the city plays host to the biggest annual jazz festival in the world every summer, it would be a mistake to call Montreal a jazz city. There's no radio station that specializes in the genre and only a couple of what could truly be called jazz clubs (the House of Jazz at 2060 rue Aylmer and Upstairs at 1254 rue Mackay).

Did you know...

that in 1851 Montreal became home to the first YMCA in North America? The Y had been founded in 1844 in London, England.

Did you know...

that the Montreal Museum of Fine Arts is the oldest public art gallery in Canada?

And yet, the city has an unmistakably jazzy history that started during Prohibition days in the United States and hit its golden age in the 1950s and '60s when Montreal was a hot stop on the jazz musicians' tour. It was particularly popular with Afro-American performers who found they could stay and eat where they wanted and date any willing female without being lynched or run out of town on a rail.

Greats from Louis Armstrong to Thelonius Monk played at such venues as the Esquire Show Bar and Rockhead's Paradise. Some of them, like bassist Charlie Biddle and drummer Walter Bacon, stayed. And the city has produced at last on authentic jazz great of its own in pianist Oscar Peterson, the son of a railway porter who became one of the most beloved musicians of the era.

Weblinks

Place des Arts
www.placedesarts.ca
Looking for the latest Place des Arts news and upcoming events? You've come to the right place. Music, dance, drama and visual arts for all ages.

Montreal Plus
www.montrealplus.ca
What's on, what's new and what's hot in the city – everything from arts and entertainment to bars and restaurants.

Montreal Jazz Festival
www.montrealjazzfest.com
The festival offers more than 400 concerts over about ten days each summer. Features of the site include the programming for the 10 days, history of the festival, photo gallery and much more.

Economy

Although Montreal was founded as a religious colony, it soon became a centre for the fur trade. The city remained little more than a colonial outpost, however, until the 19th century, when it became an important North American transportation hub. The opening of the Lachine Canal in 1825, and the Victoria Bridge in 1860 (which allowed trains on and off the island) proved vital not just for shipping and trade, but also Montreal's burgeoning manufacturing industry.

For many years Montreal was Canada's largest and most economically powerful city, with St. James Street (now known as Saint-Jacques) Canada's answer to Wall Street. Toronto began to challenge Montreal's predominance as early as early as the 1920s, and by the 1950s was a serious rival. Montreal's 1970s economic stagnation, attributed in part to the election of the Parti Québécois in 1976 and the associated threat of Québec secession, accelerated the move of economic activity westward.

Montreal's economy paled next to Toronto's for much of the 1970s and 80s. After a prolonged slump, however, Montreal staged a revival in the late 1990s and early part of this century. Montreal remains an important business center, and is second in the country in head office employment. Moreover, the Montreal economy is highly diversified with strengths in shipping and trade, garment manufacture, aerospace, biomedical research, agri-food, communications and information technology, education, culture and tourism. The city of Montreal has less than a quarter of Quebec's population, but its $93 billion in GDP (2005) represents more than 36 percent of Quebec's total.

GDP
Gross Domestic Product (GDP) represents the total value of goods and services produced.
- City of Montreal's 2005 GDP: $92.9 billion
- GDP per capita: $49,591.76
- City of Montreal's percentage of the province of Quebec's 2005 GDP: 36.2
- City of Montreal's percentage of the Quebec population of 7,669,100 (2006): 24.4

Source: Institut de la statistique Quebec.

QUEBEC TAXES
- QST (provincial sales tax): 7.5 percent
- GST (federal sales tax): 6 percent
- Personal income tax rates: 20 percent
- Small business tax rate: 8 percent
- Corporate tax rate: 11.8 percent

Source: Canada Customs and Revenue Agency.

TAX FREEDOM DAY
Tax freedom day (date on which earnings no longer go to taxes, 2007) is nationally June 19.
- Alberta: June 1
- New Brunswick: June 14
- Prince Edward Island: June 14
- Saskatchewan: June 14
- Manitoba: June 16
- British Columbia: June 16
- Ontario: June 19

- Nova Scotia: June 19
- Newfoundland and Labrador: July 1
- Quebec: July 26

Source: The Fraser Institute.

Take 5 PETER HADEKEL'S FIVE ECONOMY PROS AND CONS

Peter Hadekel is a business columnist for the *Montreal Gazette*. He has written on business and politics in Montreal and the province of Quebec for over thirty years. Hadekel is also author of a recent book on the Montreal aerospace giant Bombardier entitled *Silent Partners: Taxpayers and the Bankrolling of Bombardier*.

Five Great Things About the Montreal Economy:

1. The cost of living is among the lowest of any large city in North America.

2. The city is home to four universities and boasts the largest per capita student population in North America after Boston.

3. It's a hot place for companies to research and develop new video games.

4. The Montreal area is home to more than 50 per cent of Canada's aerospace industry.

5. If you want to start a business, there are government subsidies and tax credits galore.

5 Things To Watch Out for in the Montreal Economy

1. Quebec income taxes are among the highest in North America.

2. Red tape and government regulation cost a bundle.

3. Demographers predict serious labour shortages within 10 years as baby boomers retire.

4. The city can't hold on to new immigrants, often for language reasons.

5. Productivity is poor because, well, the sidewalk cafes are awfully enticing.

Bio THE BRONFMANS

Peter C. Newman, chronicler of Canadian tycoons, describes the Bronfmans as "the Rothschilds of the New World." The Bronfmans came to Montreal via Manitoba and Saskatchewan, where patriarch Ekiel had moved in 1889, fleeing pogroms in his native Russia.

The Bronfman sons got their start in the hotel business, but made real money as Prairie bootleggers. Sam Bronfman (1891-1971), the hard driving maverick behind the Bronfman fortune, established a beachhead in Montreal in 1916 when he bought a liquor outlet and used it to ship alcohol to the "dry" provinces in the west, and subsequently, the US.

In 1925, the Bronfmans opened their own distillery in the Montreal suburb of LaSalle. This operation's three million gallon capacity made it one of the largest in the world. The dynasty didn't take full flight, however, until 1928 when the Bronfmans merged their operations with those of Ontario's Seagram distillery.

While Samuel Bronfman may have gotten rich selling liquor to the US during Prohibition, he didn't attain the upper reaches of the North American business class until later. Sam's genius was to remove alcohol from the realm of sin and sleaze, and make it an integral part of the post Depression good life.

Seagram upped the quality of the product, maintained control over manufacture and distribution, and, most importantly, owned hundreds of key brands including Seven Crown, Chivas Regal, Gordon's gin and Captain Morgan rum.

A sign that the Bronfmans had truly arrived was the 1958 construction of Seagram's New York headquarters on Park Avenue. The building remains an icon of Modernist architecture, and was designed by the legendary Mies van der Rohe. The Seagram empire did not falter with Sam's 1971 death with son Edgar Bronfman Sr. extending the Bronfman fold to include oil and real estate holdings, piling on even more wealth.

The Bronfman luster has dimmed somewhat of late, however, as the foray of Edgar Sr.'s son, Edgar Jr., into the entertainment business has proven a failure. Edgar Jr. led the 1995 sale of Seagram's 25 percent share in DuPont; he used the funds to acquire MCA/Universal, and subsequently Polygram Records.

After a series of disastrous projects, Seagram-Universal was sold to the French utility and communications giant Vivendi in 2000 in exchange for stock. The Bronfmans incurred losses in the billions as a result of these transactions; however, Forbes Magazine reports that Edgar Sr. and his brother Charles are still worth $5.5 billion between them.

The Bronfmans are not only big money makers, they are also major philanthropists who fund numerous educational, cultural and medical research efforts in Montreal and elsewhere. The Bronfman name is liberally sprinkled about Montreal – the Samuel Bronfman Building houses McGill's Faculty of Management, the Saidye Bronfman Center on Côte St. Catherine Road is named after Sam's wife, and Charles Bronfman owned the Montreal Expos from their inception in 1969 until 1990.

Moreover, the colorful Bronfman family's exploits constitute a long running soap opera, and the clan served as inspiration for Montreal writer Mordecai Richler's 1990 novel *Solomon Gursky was Here*.

You Said How Much?

All figures are hourly and are drawn from the latest available data.

Senior managers, health, education, social services	$30.64
Software engineers	$30.64
University professors	$29.23
Senior government managers and officials	$27.95
Bricklayers	$27.52
Pharmacists	$27.44
Civil Engineers	$26.54
Commissioned police officers	$26.28
Lawyers	$26.03
School principals, elementary and secondary education	$25.38
Heavy equipment mechanics	$25.13
Specialist physicians	$25.13
Veterinarians	$24.49
Social workers	$24.48
Fire chiefs and senior firefighters	$24.10
General practitioners	$23.33
Electricians	$23.00
Financial managers	$22.49
Occupational therapists	$22.31
Financial auditors and accountants	$22.18
Secondary school teachers	$22.05
Administrators, post secondary education, vocational training	$21.67
Editors	$21.41
Registered nurses	$21.03
Plumbers	$21.00
Writers	$20.64
Elementary school teachers	$20.26
Physiotherapists	$20.13
Police officers	$18.33
Fire fighters	$17.00
Letter carriers	$17.00
Graphic designers	$16.79
Retail managers	$16.67
Medical secretaries	$15.84
Legal secretaries	$15.00
Secretaries	$13.00
Auto mechanics	$13.00

Source: Human Resources and Development Canada.

Take 5 FIVE MONTREAL SALARIES

1. **Gerald Tremblay, Mayor of Montreal**, $139,000 yearly.

2. **Saku Koivu, Captain, Montreal Canadiens hockey team**, $4.75 million USD yearly.

3. **Hunter Harrison, CEO, Canadian National Railway**, $56 million yearly (includes salary, bonuses, options and other compensation).

4. **Heather Monroe-Blum, Principal, McGill University**, $360,000 yearly.

5. **Kent Nagano, Artistic Director, Montreal Symphony Orchestra**, $50, 000 per week; 16-18 weeks yearly.
Sources: La Presse; USA Today; Globe and Mail.

PERSONAL INCOME

Per capita personal income increased in Montreal from $28,987 in 2001 to $30,267 in 2005, a 4.4 percent rise. Employment income was up over 6 percent in this period, and government transfers rose 14.5 percent; per capita investment income, however, declined 9.4 percent.

- Montreal's per capita income (2005): $30,267
- Quebec's per capita income (2005): $29,499
- Canada's per capita income (2005): $32,600
- Montreal's disposable income per capita: $23,044
- Average employment income of workers 25-64 years of age (2004): $40,998

Sources: Institut de la statistique Quebec; Fin Facts.

HOUSEHOLD INCOME

Household income in the Montreal region lags significantly behind that of other Canadian centers. The median household income in Canada after taxes was $44,100 in 2004.

Real Median Household After Tax Income for Selected Metropolitan

Take 5 FIVE KEY SECTORS IN THE METROPOLITAN MONTREAL ECONOMY

1. **Aerospace:** Montreal is home to the Canadian Space Agency as well as major private employers such as Bombardier and Pratt & Whitney. The industry comprises over 200 companies and employs 38,000. Montreal area aerospace exports totaled nine billion dollars in 2005.

2. **Life Sciences:** Over 40,000 people are employed in 628 companies and 149 public and para-public research organizations. Montreal ranks number one in Canada for research centers and academic research funding, and is eighth in North America in bio-pharmaceutical industry jobs.

3. **Information and Communication Technologies:** 110,000 people work in the industry, including 12,500 in research and development in private, public and university centers. There are 2,700 companies in Metropolitan Montreal and sales of $21 billion annually.

4. **Agri-Food:** Montreal's agri-food industry is focused on processing and distribution. There are a number of research centers based in Saint-Hyacinthe, 45 minutes from Montreal. Among the major employers is Montreal-based Suputo, Inc., which operates 46 plants worldwide and is the largest dairy processor and snack cake producer in Canada.

5. **Clothing and textile manufacturing:** Montreal's garment industry ranks second in North America behind Los Angeles. Long a major Montreal employer, the garment industry has shed jobs in recent years, but still employs about 25,000 people.

Areas (2004)
- Calgary: $56,700
- Toronto: $54,600
- Winnipeg: $45,000
- Halifax: $42,400
- Vancouver: $42,400
- Quebec City: $42,000
- **Montreal: $40,800**

Source: Canada Mortgage and Housing Corporation.

AVERAGE HOUSEHOLD EXPENDITURES IN SELECTED CANADIAN METROPOLITAN AREAS

Montreal households have low levels of expenditures compared to those in other Canadian cities. This is a reflection of lower incomes in metropolitan Montreal, as well as Montreal's relatively low cost of living. Average annual expenditures for all Canadian households are $66,857.
- Calgary: $85,553
- Toronto: $85,123
- Vancouver: $72,782
- Winnipeg: $63,525
- Halifax: $62,313
- **Montreal: $57,659**
- Quebec City: $56,789

Source: Statistics Canada.

POVERTY
- Percentage of persons defined by Statistics Canada as "low income" after taxes in Montreal in 2004: 13.7
- Average for the period 2000-2004: 16.4
- Number of welfare claimants in Montreal in 2005: 63,400
- Number of welfare claimants in Montreal in 1995: 106,200

GIMME SHELTER

Montreal has comparatively low housing costs. The average Canadian household's expenditure on shelter in 2005 was $12,614.

Average annual household expenditure on shelter in selected Canadian metropolitan areas (2005):

• Toronto: $17,771

Bio PIERRE PÉLADEAU

Pierre Péladeau (1925-1997) perfectly embodied the rise of Quebec's French-speaking business class. Until the Quiet Revolution of the early 1960s, Montreal's big firms had largely been run by anglos, with ambitious francophones restricted to the professions, education, and the Church.

Péladeau represented a new breed of Québécois entrepreneur, and Quebecor, the Montreal-based media company he founded, regularly records gross revenues of over ten billion dollars annually.

Péladeau's unbecoming looks, short stature, scrappy manner and reputation for straight talk made him something of a Québecois legend. He stepped on plenty of toes on his way to top, and was held in perhaps equal measures of respect, adoration and loathing. Bernard Bujold, Péladeau's associate and biographer, called him the Don Corleone of Quebec.

The Outremont-born Péladeau began his rise in 1950 with a $1,500 loan from his mother. He used the money to purchase a community paper in Montreal's Rosemont neighborhood, and soon acquired additional small local papers. In 1955, Péladeau launched a celebrity gossip sheet, capitalizing on the rise of the new medium of television.

Péladeau had correctly anticipated the burgeoning mass appetite for sports, celebrity and crime news, and recognized that in rapidly modernizing Montreal, francophones were no longer keen to defer to religious or political authorities. Péladeau's scored a major coup in 1964 when he launched the tabloid *Le Journal de Montreal*, which

- Calgary: $15,270
- Vancouver: $15,250
- Halifax: $12,661
- Winnipeg: $10,882
- **Montreal: $10,605**
- Quebec: $9,567

grew to be the largest French language daily in North America.

Quebecor has become a global player by adding printing and book and magazine publishing to its newspaper base. As early as the 1950s, Péladeau had been printing his own papers; Quebecor entered even more heavily into the printing business in the 1970s.

In the 1980s and 90s, Quebecor became a vertically integrated media octopus that charged far beyond Quebec's borders, establishing printing and publishing operations in a number of countries. At each step of the way, Péladeau added another piece to the media puzzle, even acquiring a major paper company in 1987 when he chafed at the high cost of pulp for his printing operations.

Quebecor, whose current President and CEO, Pierre Karl Péladeau, is founder Pierre's son, remains a printing and publishing titan. Quebecor also owns Vidéotron, (Quebec's largest cable operation and a major Internet service provider), TVA (the leading Quebec television network), Archambault Musique (Quebec's largest chain of music stores), and several high powered firms distributing books, newspapers and music in Quebec and worldwide.

Married three times and a father of seven, Péladeau had his share of personal demons – he was a recovered alcoholic and acknowledged suffering from manic depression. Pierre Péladeau is remembered as a perceptive and sometimes ruthless businessman, a major patron of the arts, as well as a supporter of causes related to substance abuse. He remade the media landscape in Quebec and elsewhere, and was emblematic of a new breed of Montreal entrepreneur.

Take 5   FIVE LEADING AREAS OF HOUSEHOLD EXPENDITURES
IN METROPOLITAN MONTREAL CENSUS AREA

1. **Personal Income Taxes:** $13,123
2. **Shelter:** $10,605
3. **Food:** $6,988
4. **Transportation:** $6,651
5. **Personal Insurance Payments & Pension Contributions:** $3,557

Source: Statistics Canada.

THE MONTREAL COMMUTE

The average Canadian spends nearly 12 full days each year traveling between home and work, which works out to approximately 63 minutes a day. The Toronto commute, the longest in Canada, is 79 minutes a day. The Montreal commute by comparison is 60 minutes.

Source: Statistics Canada.

WORK ON THE ISLAND

- Percentage who drive: 53
- Percentage who take public transportation: 33
- Walk: 8
- Passenger in a car: 4
- Bicycle: 2

Source: City of Montreal.

Did you know...

that Molson Coors Brewing Co., the world's fifth largest brewery, is the product of the 2005 merger of Molson's with Colorado-based Coors? In addition to founding Canada's first brewery in Montreal in 1786, John Molson opened Canada's first industrial grain distillery, enabling him to become a pioneer in exporting Canadian produced spirits to England.

Bombardier

Bombardier traces its roots to the most Québécois of inventions, the snowmobile. In the 1930s, Joseph-Armand Bombardier of Valcourt, Quebec (125 km east of Montreal) sought to develop a vehicle capable of "floating on snow." His invention was patented in 1937, and in the 1940s Bombardier began manufacturing the tank-like machines for military use.

Headquartered in Montreal, Bombardier now has plants world-wide and employs nearly 56,000 people with annual revenues approaching $15 billion.

The company's current size reflects its voracious acquisitions appetite in the 1980s and 90s. Bombardier gobbled up Canadair, Learjet and de Havilland, as well as a number of other big aircraft and rail manufacturers in North America and Europe. The company also developed major finance, prefab housing and business services operations.

The Bombardier firm's breakthrough came in 1959 with the debut of the Ski-Doo, which kicked off the recreational snowmobiling craze. Bombardier later diversified its operations to include rail transportation (scoring a major contract with the city of Montreal in 1974 for the manufacture of Metro cars). Bombardier has since landed a slew of train and subway car contracts, including deals with New York City, London, South Korea and the US Amtrak system. A 2003 deal to modernize London's Underground was worth $7.9 billion.

Bombardier ranks as the world's largest passenger train manufacturer, and is number three in productions of civilian aircraft. The recreational vehicles division, which produces the Ski-Doo, ATVs and Sea-Doo watercraft, was sold in 2003 to a company controlled by the Bombardier family.

The new millennium has not been kind to Bombardier – tumbling stock prices and profits, as well as job cuts in the tens of thousands, have marked the company's fortunes since 2001. 9-11 was devastating to the airline industry, and Bombardier's share prices are now in the three-dollar range, as opposed to the high of $25 recorded in 2001.

NO PARKING
- Median cost of monthly parking (unreserved rate) in Montreal: $259
- Median cost in Edmonton; $140
- Median cost in Vancouver: $194
- Median cost in Toronto: $300
- Median cost in Calgary: $375
- Canadian average: $194.51

Source: Collier's International.

WHAT MONTREALERS ARE DOING AT WORK (2006)
Employment By Sector
- Retail and wholesale sales and trade: 152,000
- Manufacturing: 123,700
- Healthcare and social assistance: 110,800
- Professional, scientific & technical services: 96,100
- Education: 73,800
- Finance, insurance, real estate: 67,500
- Information, culture, recreation: 61,800
- Accommodation and food services: 58,900
- Business, building and other support services: 47,600
- Transportation and housing: 40,100
- Other services: 39,400
- Public administration: 31,500
- Construction: 29,000
- Utilities: 4,700
- Forestry, fishing, mining, oil & gas: 2,200
- Total employment: 940,200

Source: Institut de la statistique Quebec.

Needle Trade

Montreal's garment industry ranks second in North America to Los Angeles as a center for clothing design, production, distribution and marketing. Like elsewhere in North America, the needle trade has been hard hit by Asian imports and employment has declined from 65,000 in 1999 to the mid twenty thousands in 2006.

Jewish immigrants of the early 20th century put the Montreal clothing industry on the map. Some people still speak of the rag or schmatte trade, but most in the business prefer "fashion industry." And just as in the early years of the previous century, immigrants still form a substantial portion of the Montreal clothing industry workforce.

Montreal's garment business is concentrated in the north-central and north-east parts of the city, particularly in the boroughs of Ahuntsic-Cartierville and Villeray-St. Michel-Parc Extension. Chabanel Street, north of Boulevard Métropolitain between St. Laurent and du Parc, is the heart of the Montreal needle trade and houses many production centers, design operations and showrooms.

The industry had profited from improved access to the US market following the implementation of the North American Free Trade Agreement in 1994, but a stronger Canadian dollar and the removal of global import quotas in 2005 have hurt business in the last several years.

The Montreal clothing industry, which produces everything from fur coats to jeans to lingerie, may be down, but it is certainly not out. The key, say garment business insiders, is focusing on innovative design and customer service, as well as developing market niches. Many companies are surviving by maintaining their design and marketing operations in Montreal, while outsourcing some or all production work overseas.

BUSINESSES IN MONTREAL

- Number of businesses in Montreal: 60,660
- Number of businesses in the Census Metropolitan Area: approximately 100,000
- Number employed (full and part-time) in Montreal in February 2007: 943,300
- Number unemployed in February 2007: 88,300
- Employment rate (percentage of the population holding a job): 59.3%
- Montreal's unemployment rate in February 2007: 8.6%
- Province of Quebec's unemployment rate in February 2007: 7.7%.
- Canada's unemployment rate in February 2007: 6.1%.

SMALL BUSINESS

Montreal is home to 24.5 small business per 1,000 people in Canada. Here's how other major centres compare (number per 1,000 people).

- Vancouver: 38.4
- Edmonton: 36.4
- Toronto: 28.2
- Ottawa: 27.1
- Calgary: 40.3

Sources: Emploi Quebec (Employment Quebec); City of Montreal; Institut de la statistique Quebec.

Did you know...

that Saint-Césaire, Quebec, located 60 km east of Montreal, is the North American capital of the screw top cap? Alcan Packaging employs over 100 workers in its Saint-Césaire plant, which provides over 80 percent of North America's screw top caps. Business is booming as the once tacky screw tops increasingly replace traditional corks, even in high-end wines.

LANGUAGE OF WORK

It's not uncommon to hear Montrealers rapidly switching back and forth from French to English at work. This is a matter of demographics, economics and law. Quebec's 1977 Charter of the French Language specifies a number of provisions concerning the use of French in the workplace, as well as requirements regarding French on commercial signs. 50 percent of Montreal's workforce is French/English bilingual, and 10 percent of the workforce speaks a third language.

LANGUAGES SPOKEN IN THE MONTREAL WORKPLACE

- French and English: 50.2%
- French only: 31.6%
- English only: 11.8%
- English, French and a nonofficial language: 2.9%
- French and a nonofficial language: 1.4%
- English and a nonofficial language: 1.4%
- Exclusively a language other than English or French: 0.8%

Source: City of Montreal.

SELF-EMPLOYMENT

Self-employment is a growing trend across the country. See how some of Canada's major cities compare in the be-your-own-boss category. . . (Number per 1,000)

- Calgary: 95.0
- Vancouver: 93.7
- Toronto: 76.9
- Edmonton: 75.1
- Ottawa: 69.3
- **Montreal: 67.1**

Did you know...

that Plexiglass was invented in 1931 by William Chalmers, a McGill University graduate student in chemistry?

... and in the growth rate of self-employment between 2002 and 2006:

- Calgary: 22.8 percent
- Edmonton: 22.1 percent
- **Montreal: 13.9 percent**
- Vancouver: 12.7 percent
- Toronto: 9.9 percent
- Ottawa: 2.0 percent

Source: Alberta Economic Update.

WORKING FOR THE PROVINCE

- Government of Quebec workers in Montreal (2005-06): 14,376.
- Increase since 2001-02: .8 percent
- Montreal's percentage of Government of Quebec workers: 21.3

Source: Institut de la statistique Quebec.

O/T

- Percentage of Montrealers who work more than 50 hours a week: 7
- Percentage of Edmontonians: 28
- Percentage of Calgarians: 24
- Percentage of Torontonians: 20
- Percentage of Vancouverites: 16

Source: Bank of Montreal.

Did you know...

that L' École des Hautes Études Commerciales (HEC) was Canada's first management school? HEC is affiliated with the Université de Montréal, and was founded in 1907. The school enrolls nearly 12,000 students in 33 programs. Its MBA is offered in both English and French, and attracts over half of its students from abroad.

MONTREAL, INTERNATIONAL CITY

- 60 international organizations
- 17,000 foreign students
- 85 Consulates General
- Over 70 ethno-cultural communities
- 14 foreign banks (head offices)
- 70 international organizations' headquarters (more than in all other Canadian provinces put together)
- Some 60 foreign delegations and 80 financial centre offices

Source: City of Montreal.

YOUTH ON OUR SIDE

Montreal falls in the middle when compared to other major centres in regards to the proportion of self-employed people who are ages 15-35 with 18.4 percent.

- Calgary: 20.1 percent
- Edmonton: 19.3 percent
- Ottawa: 19.2 percent
- Toronto: 17.6 percent
- Vancouver: 16.3 percent

Did you know...

that Montreal's Golden Square Mile, roughly between Atwater and Park/Bleury Streets, and Pine Avenue and Boulevard René Lévesque, was at one time home to as much as 70 percent of Canada's wealth? It now comprises much of downtown Montreal, and includes such institutions as McGill University and the Musée des Beaux Arts.

SHIPPING NEWS - THE PORT OF MONTREAL

- Tonnes of cargo handled annually: 20 million
- Rank in Canada in container traffic: 1
- Rank in North America in container traffic: 13
- Countries served: over 100
- Economic spin-offs produce: $2 billion yearly
- Direct and indirect jobs created by the port: 17,600

Source: Port of Montreal.

LEADING CANADIAN CITIES FOR HEAD OFFICE EMPLOYMENT AND PERCENTAGE OF CANADIAN TOTAL (2005)

- Toronto 59,163 – 34%
- **Montreal 36,893 – 21%**
- Calgary 19,428 – 11%
- Vancouver 11,938 – 7%
- Winnipeg 6,890 – 4%

Source: Statistics Canada.

Did you know...

that two pope-mobiles were assembled at a plant near Montreal? While John Paul II paraded around in one, the other was flown ahead to the next city on his tour.

Take 5 MONTREAL'S FIVE LARGEST PRIVATE EMPLOYERS

1. **Metro Inc:** 65,000 employees. Food retailing and distribution.
2. **Alcan Inc:** 64,900 employees. Mining and materials processing.
3. **BCE Inc:** 60,000 employees. Communications and information technology.
4. **Bombardier:** 55,800 employees. Manufacturing — air and rail transportation.
5. **Quebecor:** 47,400. Media.

Source: Globe and Mail.

DOWNTOWN OFFICE SPACE (MILLIONS OF SQUARE FEET)

- Toronto: 59.4
- **Montreal: 50.0**
- Calgary: 32.1
- Vancouver: 22.6
- Edmonton: 14.0
- Ottawa: 14.0
- Winnipeg: 12.9
- Victoria: 7.8

OFFICE VACANCY RATES (2005)

- **Montreal 13.0**
- Toronto 9.5
- Vancouver 7.5
- Calgary 5.0

Source: City of Vancouver.

Did you know...

that a Montreal taxi license fetches $230,000? There are 4,500 licensed Montreal taxicabs and nearly 10,000 drivers.

COST OF OFFICE SPACE

Montreal's metro area office space is very affordable at $31.78 per square foot, compared to $46.06 in Toronto and $47.58 in Calgary.

Source: Montreal International.

BUILDING PERMIT VALUES

City	Jan-Jun 2006	Jan-Jun 2007
Toronto	$5.0 billion	$6.2 billion
Vancouver	$3.0 billion	$3.8 billion
Montreal	**$2.87 billion**	**$3.2 billion**
Calgary	$2.4 billion	$3.5 billion
Ottawa/Gatineau	$1.1 billion	$1.2 billion

Source: Statistics Canada.

They Said It

"I love competition. Without it you can't be in this game. You might as well live on top of a mountain and write poetry. If you don't keep driving, you'll fall back. And that's just not in us."

– Edgar Bronfman Sr.

Did you know...

that the Montreal Stock Exchange, Canada's first, was established in 1874? Informal trading had been occurring as early as 1832 when brokers used the Exchange Coffee House as a venue to swap shares. The Montreal Stock Exchange obtained its own building in 1904 — that structure is now the home of the Centaur Theatre Company.

DOWNTOWN MONTREAL

- Number of stores: 6,000
- Number of major shopping complexes: 10
- Number of dining spots: 6,516
- Number of department stores: 6
- Number of movie theatres: 59
- Number of historic spots: 35
- Number of tourist attractions: 80-100
- Number major festivals each year: 40
- Number public spaces/parks: 1,222
- Number of parking spots: 40,000
- Number of hotel rooms: 15,200

Sources: Tourism Montreal; City of Montreal.

Did you know...

that Montreal receives over seven million overnight visitors annually? The average overnight visitor stays 2.89 nights and spends $330.59. Tourism is responsible for over 73,000 jobs in the Montreal area.

Did you know...

that there are 8,000 retail businesses in Montreal employing 111,000 workers?

THE FUR TRADE

Montreal remains a center for fur garment production, and is home to the Fur Council of Canada.

- Montreal's share of Canadian fur garment manufacturing: 80 percent
- Number of firms in Montreal making fur and leather clothing: 96
- Workers employed in fur and leather manufacture in Montreal: 767
- Fur and leather workers as a percentage of employment in Montreal's garment industry: 3

Sources: Fur Council of Canada; McGill University; City of Montreal.

Did you know...

that McGill University's Office of Development and Alumni Relations now occupies Seagram's former Peel Street headquarters in downtown Montreal? Sam Bronfman himself chose the site for the 1928 building, whose facade is modeled after a 16th Century Scottish castle. The building was given to McGill in 2002 by Vivendi Universal, Seagram's owners, at the behest of the Bronfman family.

Weblinks

Board of Trade of Metropolitan Montreal

www.btmm.qc.ca/asp/contenu.asp?lang=2&GrSection=7

The voice of the Montreal area business community, both anglophone and francophone. Contains a wide range of data and information about the Montreal economy, as well as other aspects of life in the city.

Metropolitan Montreal Community

www.cmm.qc.ca/index.php?id=309

Metropolitan Montreal Community site includes data and information about the metro area, including economic development, infrastructure and transportation.

Montreal International

www.montrealinternational.com/en/accueil/index.asp

Promotes economic development in Montreal and the city's profile internationally.

Montreal Economic Institute

www.iedm.org/main/main.php

Research and educational institute based on a collaboration of academics, entrepreneurs and economists. The MEI promotes "an economic approach to the study of public policy issues."

Politics

There has been some form of politics in Montreal ever since De Maisoneuve founded the city in 1640. When most territories belonging to New France were ceded to the English in 1763, it merely created a new and peculiar brand of politics that is unique to Montreal and Quebec.

French Montrealers had to deal with a city that had suddenly been ceded to a foreign and one time hostile crown. Large-scale immigration of people of British origin only complicated matters further. Conflict between French and English and struggles for representative government marked the 1830s and resulted in the rebellions of 1837. The defeat of the patriotes, however, gave new political impetus to a period detente.

Montreal civic government has had its black periods. Early city councillors like Raymond Préfontaine built tremendous political power handing out municipal contracts to friends in late 1890s, power he rode all the way to the mayor's office. The practice of telegraphing, voting under someone else's name (even a dead someone else) was widespread before and after him.

Meanwhile, whole books have been written on just how crooked a town Montreal was in the 1940s and '50s, with a number of policemen and other city officials on the payroll of local crime organizations. The party system did not emerge at the municipal level until the early-1950s.

> *"Your majesty, I thank you from the bottom of my heart, and Madame Houde here thanks you from her bottom too."*
> **– Mayor Camilien Houde Speaking to King George VI in 1939.**

MEGA CITY

The idea of bringing together all of the far-flung suburbs of Montreal under the rubric of one super-city is an idea that had been floated since the Drapeau years. When Montreal mayor Pierre Bourque came to power, the idea was put forth again, this time with the backing of the provincial government, which wanted bigger, more efficient cities modelled after other cities in North America which had done the same thing.

Bourque called his idea of unifying the 27 municipalities on the Island of Montreal "Une Île, Une Ville" (One Island, One City). Although he was reelected in 1998 in the early days of the One Island initiative, the decision to pursue it cost both Bourque and the provincial government their next term. Most of the island suburbs had little time for the idea and protested vehemently.

The voters tossed out Bourque in November 2001, electing former provincial Liberal MNA Gerald Tremblay and his Montreal Island Citizens Union. At this point, however, there appeared to be no turning back, and the new super-city became a reality on January 1, 2002. The former suburbs and existing districts became boroughs represented by borough mayors.

The demerger process begun in 2003 was a complicated one. Suburbs

Did you know...

that Henry Archer Ekers, the 28th mayor of Montreal, was the last Anglophone to hold that position? Ever since Peter McGill followed Jacques Viger into the mayor's office, the mayoralty of Montreal had alternated between Francophones and Anglophones. The practice ended with Ekers, mayor from 1906 to 1908.

They Said It

"You know, some of that cheering is for you too."
– Mayor Houde commenting on cheering crowds to King George VI and Queen Elizabeth during their 1939 visit to Montreal.

that wanted autonomy first had to hold referendums on whether or not to hold referendums. Twenty-two of them did, fifteen of which chose to regain their independence.

CITY GOVERNMENT

As of January 1, 2006, when formerly merged suburbs officially demerged (15 former suburbs on the island of Montreal demerged) from the city of Montreal, the new political landscape included 19 boroughs administered by 105 elected officials (one mayor, 19 borough mayors, 45 city councillors and 40 borough councillors).

A newly created Agglomeration Council is responsible for overseeing traditional city services (police and fire services, drinking and waste water treatment, and property assessments) to the other municipalities on the Island of Montreal. The council consists of 16 elected officials from the city of Montreal and 15 elected officials – one from each of the "reconstituted" municipalities.

As of January 1st, 2006, the Island of Montreal was made up of 16 municipalities, including the city of Montreal, Baie D'Urfé, Beaconsfield, Côte-Saint-Luc, Dollard-des-Ormeaux Dorval, Hampstead, Kirkland, L'Île-Dorval, Montréal-Est, Montréal-Ouest, Mont-Royal, Pointe-Claire, Sainte-Anne-de-Bellevue, Senneville and Westmount.

They Said It

"The Olympics can no more have a deficit than a man can have a baby."
– Montreal Mayor Jean Drapeau, 1973.

Take 5   ALAN HUSTAK'S FIVE MOST MEMORABLE MONTREAL MAYORS

Over the last four decades, veteran journalist Alan Hustak has covered just about everything in Montreal for the CBC, CTV and the *Montreal Gazette*. He is also the author of nine books, including *Montreal Then and Now*, *The Ghost of Griffintown: The True Story of the Murder of Mary Gallagher*, and a biography of Montreal Mayor Sir William Hingston.

1. **The Best:** Arguably, Dr. William Hingston, who in his two terms in the 1870s bridged secular, religious and political divisions to save thousands of lives by forcing residents to be inoculated against smallpox, and used his diplomatic skills to avert bloody civil strife during what was known as the Guibord Affair — an ongoing political crisis between French Roman Catholics and English Protestants over the burial in a Roman Catholic cemetery of a printer who had been excommunicated for his liberal views. Hingston is also responsible for the construction of Mount Royal Park. As chief surgeon at the Hôtel Dieu Hospital, he helped lay the groundwork for what is today Université de Montréal. He was later appointed to the Canadian Senate and knighted by Queen Victoria.

2. **The Most Dictatorial:** Jean Drapeau, elected eight times between 1954 and 1986, with overwhelming majorities. Drapeau was the last of a breed of so called North American "boss" mayors who crushed all opposition and who transformed their cities by force of sheer willpower. Drapeau always maintained that "democracy isn't a system of public participation, but a system where voters choose leaders to do things. What I believe is dangerous is opposition on a day-to-day basis." Drapeau put Montreal on the map, introduced lotteries to Canada, gave the city its métro, the 1967 World's Fair and the 1976 Summer Olympic Games. He also left it in debt with a billion-dollar hangover.

3. **The Most Outrageous:** Camillien Houde, who served seven terms between 1928 and 1954, had three separate wardrobes to accommodate his corpulent 300 pound frame. Houde was ebullient, mischevious, provocative, defiant and sometimes vulgar. When he participated in the 1950 Grey Cup kickoff in Toronto, he cheerfully declared, "It's always a pleasure for me to kick your balls off."

If he is remembered at all it is for the wrong reason – he was jailed for treason during the Second World War for urging Montrealers not to register for conscription. When he was released from prison in 1944, Montrealers not only re-elected him as their mayor, but also elected him to the House of Commons in Ottawa as the MP for Papineau. A mayor who combined his devout Roman Catholicism with a touch of hedonism, Houde once remarked so long as Montrealers kept a healthy balance between the praying and the sinning, the city would never sink into wickedness.

4. **The Most Eccentric:** Charles-Séraphin Rodier. Not only did he spend one-quarter of the city's finances to welcome the Prince of Wales for the opening of the Victoria Bridge in 1860, Rodier had robes trimmed with ermine made for himself and commissioned a gold chain of office as well as a replica of the sword carried by the Lord Mayor of London. He christened his house Chateau Prince of Wales and had a statue of the future king installed on a turret. He insisted he be addressed as 'your highness' instead of 'your worship.' Small wonder his opponents nicknamed him "The Peacock," and he lost the 1862 election.

5. **The Nearest to Sainthood:** John Easton Mills, Montreal's first mayor of Irish descent, took office in 1846. Mills came to Montreal from Massachusetts, where he was born in 1796, to work in the fur trade. He became a banker, and during the typhus epidemic that hit Montreal in the summer of 1847, shortly after he took office, he personally volunteered to look after the sick and dying. He exhausted himself and died of the contagious disease in November 1847.

Did you know...

that Montreal was named the capital of Canada in 1843 but held the distinction for just two years?

TOTAL OPERATING BUDGETS APPROVED BY MONTREAL CITY COUNCIL
- 2006: $3.855 billion
- 2007: $3.92 billion

Mayors of Montreal

Name	Term	Profession
Jacques Viger	1833-1836	Newspaperman/Author/Civil Servant
Peter McGill	1840-1842	Businessman
Joseph Bourret	1842-1844 and 1847-1849	Lawyer
James Ferrier	1844-1846	Merchant/Businessman
John Easton Mills	1846-1847	Fur Merchant/Banker
Edouard-Raymond Fabre	1849-1851	Bookseller
Charles Wilson	1851-1854	Businessman
Wolfred Nelson	1854-1856	Doctor
Henry Starnes	1856-1858 and 1866-1868	Merchant/Banker
Charles-Seraphin Rodier	1858-1862	Merchant/Lawyer/Philanthropist
Jean-Louis Beaudry	1862-1866/1877-1879/1881-1885	Entrepreneur
William Workman	1868-1871	Businessman
Charles-Joseph Coursol	1871-1873	Lawyer/Businessman
Francis Cassidy	1873	Lawyer
Aldis Bernard	1873-1875	Dentist
William Hales Hingston	1875-1877	Doctor/Surgeon
Severe Rivard	1879-1881	Lawyer/Businessman
Honore Beaugrand	1885-1887	Journalist/Newspaper Owner
John Caldwell Abbott	1887-1888	Lawyer/Businessman
Jacques Grenier	1889-1891	Businessman
James McShane	1891-1893	Businessman

HIGH COST OF GOVERNMENT (2006)

In 2006 it cost the city $3.29 billion to operate. The biggest single expense was policing, which cost over $488 million. Here's where the rest was spent:

- General administration $478.8 million
- Financing Expenses: $400.9 million
- Public Transit: $320.8 million
- Recreational Activities: $268.4 million
- Fire Safety: $263.9 million

Name	Term	Profession
Alphonse Desjardins	1893-1894	Journalist/Lawyer/ Businessman
Joseph-Octave Villeneuve	1894-1896	Businessman
Richard Wilson-Smith	1896-1898	Journalist/Financier
Raymond Prefontaine	1898-1902	Lawyer
James Cochrane	1902-1904	Contractor
Hormidas Laporte	1904-1906	Financier/Businessman
Henry Archer Ekers	1906-1908	Industrialist
Louis Payette	1908-1910	Contractor
James John Edmund Guerin	1910-1912	Doctor
Louis-Arsene Lavallee	1912-1914	Lawyer
Mederic Martin	1914-1924 and 1926-1928	Industrialist
Charles Duquette	1924-1926	Businessman
Camillien Houde	1928-32/ 1934-36/ 1938-40/1944-54	Banker
Fernand Rinfret	1932-1934	Journalist
Adhemar Raynault	1936-1938 and 1940-1944	Businessman
Jean Drapeau	1954-1957 and 1960-1986	Lawyer
Sarto Fournier	1957-1960	Lawyer
Jean Dore	1986-1994	Journalist
Pierre Bourque	1994-2001	Horticulturist
Gerald Tremblay	2001-present	Lawyer

- Water and sewage: $172.6 million
- Urban planning and development: $157.1 million
- Cultural activities: $150.5 million
- Waste removal and recycling: $142.2 million
- Public housing, income security, community health: $124.8 million
- Municipal roads: $118.6 million
- Snow removal: $107.2 million
- Traffic and parking: $37.1 million
- Other: $32.7 million
- City lighting: $28.4 million

WHERE MONTREAL GETS ITS CASH (PERCENT)
- Total revenues: $3.77 billion
- Taxes: $2.53 billion
- Payments in lieu of taxes: $246.3 million
- Other revenues from local sources: $636.5 million
- Transfers: $434.6 million

FIRST MAYOR

The Viger building (Edifice Viger) and Viger Square, both on busy Viger St., are named for Jacques Viger, the first mayor of Montreal. Born in Montreal in 1787, Viger was a journalist, historian, writer, militia officer and, starting in 1813, a civil servant. In pre-charter Montreal, he surveyed roads and bridges and even conducted a census in 1825.

When he was chosen as mayor in 1833, he was responsible for adopting the city seal, the improvement of the city's lighting and drainage sys-

Did you know...

that the shortest term as Montreal mayor was served by Frederick Cassidy, the city's 14th mayor? Elected in February 1873, he died on June 14 – just three months after taking office. He was 46.

tems, and the adoption of cholera prevention measures.

Viger's political career ended in 1836 when the city's charter was revoked amid the turbulence of the Rebellions. It didn't help Viger that he was a cousin to Patriotes leader Louis-Joseph Papineau and was believed to be sympathetic to the cause.

In 1843, Viger helped form the Société St. Jean Baptiste, and later presided over the first St. Jean Baptiste celebrations to protest British tyranny. In 1858, the same year he died, he helped found the Société d' histoire de Montréal (Montreal Historical Society).

PROPERTY TAXES

Based on a sample house as defined as a 25 to 30 year-old detached 3-bedroom bungalow with a main floor area of 1,200 square feet, finished full basement and a double car garage, on a 6,000 square foot lot. Utility charges include telephones, power, water, sewer, land drainage and garbage collection.

- Ottawa $4,659
- Toronto $4,624
- Saskatoon $4,487
- Vancouver $4,216
- Regina $4,184
- St. John's $4,082
- Edmonton $3889
- Calgary $3708
- Fredericton $3, 694
- **Montreal $3,644**
- Winnipeg $3,577
- Halifax $3,402

Source: City of Edmonton, 2006 comparison report.

Bio JEAN DRAPEAU

Lawyer Jean Drapeau was Montreal's mayor for 29 years. He swept into power in 1954, won eight out of nine elections, and only retired in 1986. During his reign, Drapeau saw seven prime ministers and nine Quebec premiers come and go. He is remembered for transforming Montreal into a world-class city, providing it with Expo 67 (which drew 50 million visitors), the 1976 Summer Olympic Games, the metro system and a major league baseball team.

Drapeau also refused to fluoridate the water system, was blamed in a national inquiry for going drastically over budget for the Olympics, and only watched as Toronto supplanted Montreal as the business capital of Canada.

Brian McKenna, in his biography of Jean Drapeau wrote, "He reformed the electoral system and modernized the police department, but ignored or skirted issues such as public housing, city planning and pollution control. In 1987, Montréal was still dumping raw sewage into the St. Lawrence, much the same as it had when the city was founded in 1642."

A staunch federalist, he replied to French President Charles de Gaulle's separatist slogan "Vive le Quebec libre" with: "Quebecer's identities were forged in the Canadian cauldron, not in that of Mother France."

Despite being known for his sense of humour, Drapeau was driven by his vision of Montreal. He was a workaholic. He personally answered all his correspondence and would drive every day through Montreal, with Wagner arias blaring in his ear as he inspected the city. Following his death in 1999, his biographer McKenna said that a formal memorial of Drapeau may not be necessary because "Montreal as it exists today is the real monument to the man."

VALUATIONS

The total value of the 435,190 properties in the Montreal agglomeration reached a record level of $188 billion in 2007, compared with $129.2 billion in 2003, representing an increase in property wealth of nearly 39 percent.

PROVINCIAL AND FEDERAL REPRESENTATION FROM MONTREAL

- Provincial Legislature: 28
- Canadian House of Commons: 24

FIRST FEMALE COUNCILLORS

The 1940 election saw the first woman elected to Montreal council. Jessie Kathleen Fisher, the daughter of real estate entrepreneur Roswell Corse Fisher and a graduate of Trafalgar Institute and Miss Edgar's and Miss Cramp's School, was a elected a Class A (elected by land owners) councillor for Montreal's District 4, which was made up of the Côté Des Neiges district and parts of downtown. In 1947, Fisher became the first woman to preside over a city council meeting when she stood in for another councillor who himself was standing in for mayor Camilien Houde. She was joined in council by Class C (appointed by a committee) councillor Elisabeth Mont.

FIRST ELECTED MAYOR

In 1852, when the people were finally allowed to choose a mayor (mayors had been appointed by the council until that point), their choice was standing mayor Charles Wilson, the Scottish-born entrepreneur appointed mayor by council in 1851. He was elected mayor again in 1853. Wilson's final term in office was marred by the infamous Gavassi Riots, which occurred after popular anti-papist and former Catholic monk Alessandro Gavassi spoke at the Zion Church at Haymarket (Victoria

They Said It

"What the masses want are monuments."

– Jean Drapeau

They Said It

Square). Fighting broke out, and shots were fired by members of the militia after Wilson's reading of the Riot Act failed to cool passions. Nine people were killed and another 30 or so were injured.

Politics of Language

Language has been a subject of debate in Montreal for more than four hundred years. After France formally gave up its ambitions in North America in 1763, francophones in Quebec were more less left to defend themselves. When Lord Durham recommended assimilation in 1839 (in his report, he says he found "two nations warring in the bosom of a single state"), francophones responded with more and more babies . . . the revenge of the cradle.

In the early days of Montreal's history, shifting tides of immigration left the linguistic future of the city very much up for grabs. The English were the majority well into the 1830s. The tide began to shift, however, with rural francophone immigration to the city. Today, of course, Montreal has a decidedly French majority.

Montreal is indeed the largest French-speaking city in the world besides Paris, but it has a complicated linguistic history. In Montreal, there will probably always be linguistic tension. Strangely enough, however, Montreal is the most bilingual city in the country, and becoming more
and more so each year.

An understanding of the political history of language in the city is essential to understanding Montreal. To the outsider and many Montrealers, there is a level of absurdity attached to the to and fro of language. If you stay long enough, you will understand that absurdity as well.

LANGUAGE 101

After the Government of Canada moved to make the country official-ly bilingual in 1969, the Quebec Government passed and implement-ed several language laws that have had an impact on Montreal. In 1974, the province passed a law known as the Official Languages Act, which made French the province's sole official language. Since then, Quebec has implemented 1977's Bill 101 (the Charter of French Language), which sought to make French not only the official lan-guage of the province and its government and laws, but also the "everyday language of work, instruction, communication, business and commerce." In particular, Bill 101 made French the language for immi-grants by requiring immigrants to send their children to school in French. The law has been a leading reason for increasing the French fact in the Montreal region.

The law also more or less banned English from commercial signs, earning it several legal challenges over the years. To address the sign issue, the government of Quebec enacted Bill 178, the first of Quebec's "sign laws," which allowed English indoors but not outdoors. After a United Nations Human Rights Committee ruled that it violated civil and political rights, the government responded with Bill 86, a law requiring French lettering to be at least twice the size of any English on a sign.

Quebec even has its own language police, the Office de la langue française — aka the Tongue Troopers — to ensure that nobody dare sneak big English letters on a sign.

DIRTIEST ELECTION

The 1957 vote was the most bitterly fought election in Montreal history. The Montreal underworld, determined to put the reforming Drapeau out of business, threw their considerable and fearsome weight behind the Great Montreal Rally and its mayoral candidate Sarto Fournier.

The campaign was marked by violence, vandalism and defamation, most directed at Drapeau and his supporters, with election day itself marred by acts of intimidation, ballot box stuffing and theft. Fournier defeated

Drapeau, but the Civic Action league held a 33-21 majority in council. Drapeau left the Civic Action league shortly before the 1960 election, emerging victorious at the head of his new Civic Party of Montreal.

STICKS AND STONES AND TRUDEAU'S BONES

Federal politics and Quebec nationalism clashed on the streets of Montreal in 1968. Invited by mayor Jean Drapeau to attend the St. Jean Baptiste Parade on June 24, 1968, Prime Minister Pierre Trudeau became the target, literally, of Quebec separatists angry with the young PM and his federalist policies.

Things got ugly about an hour into the parade, when demonstrators managed to halt the procession and overturned and set fire to three police cars. When a bottle was thrown into the reviewing stand he sat in with Drapeau and Premier Johnson, Drapeau and Johnson fled to safety. Trudeau, urged to leave by his security guards, refused. Defiant, he stayed until the last float had passed. He easily won his first election the next day.

Weblinks

Quebec's Government Portal
www.gouv.qc.ca/portail/quebec/?lang=en
Official site of the government of Quebec, with information about all of its services and programs.

Montreal's City Hall
ville.montreal.qc.ca/portal/page?_pageid=66,261592&_dad=portal&_schema=PORTAL
Take a tour of the virtual council, check out the mayor's latest doings, follow up on key issues and read about democratic life.

Then and Now

Montreal's strategic location in the St. Lawrence River at the confluence of several waterways soon made it a natural fur trading centre. Once peace was established with the Iroquois, the population slowly increased, and by the 1800s Montreal was expanding rapidly. Montreal has also added to its population over the years by annexing a number of adjacent towns and villages.

The composition of its population has changed significantly over time. Montreal was nearly completely French speaking when the British took formal possession of New France in 1763. In the early 1800s, there was substantial immigration from England, Scotland and Ireland, and Montreal became a majority English-speaking city.

By the mid 1860s the balance shifted back to Francophones as many rural French speakers moved from the Quebec countryside into the city. In the 20th century, the dominance of French continued, however, the city became increasingly multicultural and multilingual, as East European Jews and Southern Europeans, notably Italians, established themselves in Montreal.

Since the 1960s, Montreal has become a truly cosmopolitan city and now has important communities hailing from a number of nations in Asia, the Middle East, North Africa and the Americas. According to the 2001 census, there were 622,000 foreign born people living in the Montreal metro area. Census Canada also reports that in 2001, French was the mother tongue of 2.27 million people in Metro Montreal, English that of 408,000, English and French 30,000, and languages other than French or English 667,000.

POPULATION
- 1651 50
- 1672 1,500
- 1763 5,200
- 1789 5,500
- 1825 22,540
- 1844 44,591
- 1861 90,000
- 1871 107,225
- 1901 267,730
- 1911 468,000
- 1921 618, 500
- 1931 818,500; Island 992,000
- 1941 903,007; Island 1,116,800; Metro Area 1,139,921
- 1951 1,021,520; Island 1,320,232; Metro Area 1,395,400
- 1961 1,191,062; Island 1,747,696; Metro Area 2,109,509
- 1971 1,214,352; Island 1,959,143; Metro Area 2,743,208
- 1981 980,354; Island 1,760,122; Metro Area 2,828,349
- 1996 1,016,376; Island 1,775,846; Metro Area 3,326,510
- 2006 1,620,693 (Merged City); 1,854,442 (Agglomeration of Montreal); Metro Area 3,635,571

Source: Montreal: A History; Ancestry.com; Heritage Montreal.

Did you know...

the cholera epidemic of 1832 killed as many as 4,500 Montrealers, about one sixth of the population?

Take 5 FIVE FAMOUS MONTREAL HOTELS, PAST AND PRESENT

1. **New Mansion House Hotel/British American Hotel** (1824-1833). Saint-Paul Street, Old Montreal. John Molson built the famed hotel on the site of the original Mansion House Hotel which was destroyed by fire in 1821. The 1,500 seat Théâtre Royal was added in 1825 and staged Shakespeare plays among other spectacles. Charles Dickens performed three different roles in an 1842 performance. The British Americans burned it down in 1833; the theatre moved to a new location in the 1840s, and its building was demolished to make way for the Bonsecours Market building.

2. **Windsor Hotel** (1878-1981). 1170 Peel, corner René Lévesque. The traditional home away from home for Royals on their visits to Canada, the Windsor also hosted Mark Twain, Oscar Wilde, Winston Churchill, Charles de Gaulle and countless others. A part of the original structure still remains and is used as an office building.

3. **Mount Royal Hotel** (1922-mid 1980s). 1455 Peel Street, corner St. Catherine. At one time the largest hotel in the British Empire, the Mount Royal boasted 1,100 rooms. Part of the hotel has been reincarnated as Les Cours Mont Royal, a four level shopping centre devoted to upscale fashion. Les Cours has retained parts of the original structure, and includes the massive chandelier that once graced the lobby.

4. **The Ritz Carlton** (1912-). 1228 Sherbrooke Street West, corner Drummond. Fittingly located in the heart of Montreal's Golden Square Mile, the Ritz has long symbolized luxury and elegance. Guests have included Mary Pickford and Douglas Fairbanks, as well as countless blue bloods, power brokers and well-heeled tourists. Liz Taylor and Richard Burton were married at the Ritz in 1964.

5. **Fairmont Queen Elizabeth** (1958-). 900 Boulevard René Lévesque. Fidel Castro was the first guest, and in 1969 John Lennon and Yoko Ono recorded "Give Peace a Chance" in room 1742. The Queen E served as headquarters of the 1976 Olympics, and hosted 50 of the 60 visiting foreign heads of state at Expo 67.

MONTREAL'S STRONGMEN

From its earliest days as gateway to the Canadian frontier, Montreal has produced a number of legendary strongmen. Montreal born Jos Montferrand (1802-1864) was a lumberjack, adventurer, fur trapper and boxer. His fellow Québécois working in lumber camps and mills across North America spread tales of Montferrand's superhuman exploits.

Montferrand was exceptionally tall for the 1800s, standing nearly 2 m (six feet four inches). For many years he toiled as a lumberjack in the Outaouais (present day Ottawa) region, where he was a fierce defender of his fellow French Canadians.

It is said that Montferrand could lift a plow with one hand, and that he took on 150 Irishmen in a fight at the Chaudières bridge near Hull, Quebec. Montferrand was lauded by Wilfred Laurier, who cited his great bravery and strength, and called the giant from Montreal "the most truly Canadian of all Canadians ever known."

Montferrand graced a Canadian postage stamp in 1992, and has been the subject of a novel, a musical, and a famed Gilles Vigneault song. At the corner of St. Catherine and Frontenac streets, lies a park named in his honor.

LOUIS CYR

Louis Cyr (1863-1912) has been called the "Strongest Man Who Ever Lived." Cyr was one of the world's first competitive weight lifters and gained global fame for an 1889 exhibition in London, England in which he lifted 250 kg with one finger, and then raised 124 kg above his head with one hand. Cyr is also credited with the greatest weight lifting feat ever – an 1895 Boston stunt in which he lifted a 1,935 kg platform holding eighteen men.

Other Cyr feats included his resisting the pull of four horses (he held two in each hand) in Montreal in 1891. Like Montferrand, Cyr was a lumberjack, but later served as a circus performer, Montreal policeman, and tavern owner (he tossed full kegs of beer about the establishment). Cyr succumbed to kidney disease in Montreal in 1912 at age 49. There is a statue of Cyr in Montreal's St. Henri district at the intersection of St. Jacques, St. Antoine and de Courcelle streets. Parc Louis Cyr is a few blocks away on St. Ferdinand Street south of Notre Dame.

THE GREAT ANTONIO

Montferrand and Cyr are the stuff of history books, but many contemporary Montrealers have seen the Great Antonio (1925-2003) in action. Born in Yugoslavia, the Great Antonio (officially Anton Barichievich) moved to Montreal in the 1940s and made his living as a traveling strongman. He appeared on *Ed Sullivan*, *The Tonight Show* and *Real People*, as well as in the movie *Quest for Fire*. Antonio, wearer of a size 28 shoe, was an immense and strange looking man – nearly 2 metres tall and weighing of 225 kg (almost 500 pounds), he had thick matted hair and a long beard.

He pulled four buses loaded with passengers along St. Catherine Street in 1960, and appears in the Guinness Book of World Records for a 1952 feat in which he hauled a train weighing 433 tonnes along 20 metres of Montreal track. Antonio was a freelancer and oddball who would spontaneously hitch a chain to a Montreal bus and start dragging it up a hill.

Prone to cryptic utterances, the illiterate Antonio dressed in rags and in his later years would use his matted dreadlocks to play "hair golf." Antonio peddled postcards of himself in a Rosemont Dunkin' Donuts outlet, as well as in the Berri-UQAM metro station. A proposal for a monument of Antonio, to be crafted by leading Quebec sculptor Armand Vaillancourt and displayed in Beaubien Park, attracted support among local residents, but did not find favour among the politicians needed to make it a reality.

Take 5 ORIGINS OF FIVE
MONTREAL STREET NAMES

1. **Sherbrooke Street.** The Golden Square Mile's elegant through-fare is named after Sir John Coape Sherbrooke (1764-1830) who was Governor in Chief of British North America from 1816-1818. Previously, Sherbrooke served as Lieutenant Governor of Nova Scotia and defended the colony during the War of 1812. The city of Sherbrooke, Quebec is also named after Sir John.

2. **De Maisonneuve Boulevard.** The downtown street is home to a number of glass office towers. Paul de Chomedy, Sieur de Maisonneuve (1612-1676) is considered the founder of Ville Marie, which in time came to be known as Montreal. De Maisonneuve arrived in late 1641 and began construction on a permanent settlement in 1642.

3. **Papineau Street.** A major artery in the east central part of Montreal, it becomes the Papineau Autoroute north of the city heading to Laval, and leads into the Jacques Cartier Bridge on its south end. Louis-Joseph Papineau was born in Montreal in 1786. A lawyer, landowner and politician, Papineau demanded that Lower Canada, as Quebec was then known, gain greater control of its own affairs. Papineau was an early exponent of French Canadian nationalism, and as result of his suspected role in the Rebellions of 1837, was forced into exile in the US and France.

4. **Peel Street.** The intersection of Peel and St. Catherine is generally acknowledged as the heart of downtown Montreal. Sir Robert Peel (1788-1850) twice served as British Prime Minister in the 1830s and 1840s.

5. **Jean Talon Street.** Home to the Jean Talon Market, the multiethnic street teems with immigrants from around the world. Jean Talon (1625-1694) was the first intendant of New France, serving from 1665 to 1668 and from 1670 to 1672. Talon is also considered Canada's original statistician and conducted North America's first census in 1665-66.

ETHNIC ORIGINS OF MONTREAL'S POPULATION

Ethnic Group	1901	1961
Chinese/Japanese	718	4,139
Other Asian	n/a	3,972
British	75,784	147,686

Bibles and Bandages

Jeanne Mance (1606-1673) and Marguerite Bourgouys (1620-1700) laid the foundations for health and education in Montreal. Mance, a nurse, is considered by many to have co-founded Ville-Marie (later called Montreal) with Paul Chomedy de Maisonneuve. She established Montreal's first hospital, Hôtel-Dieu, whose initial building was erected in 1645 at the corner of Saint-Paul and Saint-Sulpice Streets.

One of North America's first hospitals, Hôtel-Dieu had beds for six men and two women, and was encircled by a trench and stockade. Mance worked tirelessly healing the sick, as well as supporting the work of the missionaries. She was essential to the settlement's early survival, and made several trips to France to raise funds to support the fledgling religious colony. Mance died in Montreal in 1673 with fellow pioneer Marguerite Bourgeouys at her side.

Margeuerite Bourgeoys was an ally and friend of Mance in developing Montreal as a permanent settlement. Bourgeouys arrived in New France in 1653, and opened a school for girls in a converted Montreal stable in 1658. While in France, Bourgeoys had been a non-cloistered member of the Congrégation de Notre-Dame. She brought her religious convictions with her to Ville Marie, founding Notre Dame de Bonsecours Chapel in 1655.

Bourgeoys went on to establish a farm in Pointe-Saint-Charles where the filles de Roys were housed and educated. The filles were orphans in French religious institutions who were sent overseas to serve as brides for the bachelors of New France. Bourgeoys was a teacher, religious leader, social worker and administrator. She played a key role in the development of generations of young women, French and native, and has been referred to as the "Mother of the Colony." Bourgeouys was canonized by Pope John Paul II in 1982.

ETHNIC ORIGINS OF MONTREAL'S POPULATION (CONT.)

Ethnic Group	1901	1961
French	114,245	793,599
German	2,021	13,858
Italian	1,398	79,841
Dutch	102	2,233
Scandinavian	444	2,864
Russian	134	7,726

Take 5 VICTORIA DICKENSON'S FAVOURITE ARTIFACTS
AT MCCORD MUSEUM

Victoria Dickenson, Ph.D., FCMA, is Executive Director, McCord Museum of Canadian History in Montreal. She is a graduate of the Master in Museum Studies Programme at the University of Toronto and obtained her Doctorate in Canadian history from Carleton University in 1995. She has a deep and abiding passion for the actual 'stuff' of history, the objects that preserve and document our past. McCord houses over 125,000 objects, thousands of letters, diaries, scrapbooks, and journals, plus over 1,200,000 images in the Notman Photographic Archives.

1. The guest books from the Windsor Hotel. Fifty years ago, the Windsor was the place to see and to be seen, and the guest books reflect its social cachet: princes, ambassadors, foreign delegates, bishops, prime ministers, and even kings and queens, including Eleanor Roosevelt, Queen Elizabeth II and Prince Philip, Mackenzie King, Lester B. Pearson and, of course, some aristocrats of the rink, like Jean Béliveau.

2. A pair of girl's boots, dating from the late 1860s, with the name of the manufacturer, the Canadian Rubber Co. of Montreal, stamped on the soles. Rubber degrades very easily, so these boots from such an early date are very rare. Even rarer is the moose hair design embroidered by a Huron-Wendat artist on the uppers, making these boots an exceptional example of Aboriginal artistry and a Victorian fashion statement.

ETHNIC ORIGINS OF MONTREAL'S POPULATION (CONT.)

Ethnic Group	1901	1961
Ukrainian	n/a	9,199
Polish	n/a	17,210
Jewish	6,639	46,519
Aboriginal	53	507
Others	606	3,190
African-Canadian	191	2,695

Sources: Statistics Canada.

3. A painting by the Irish artist James Duncan, who came to Montreal in 1830 and painted this magnificent view of the city from the mountain shortly after his arrival. The newspaper La Minerve reported on March 3, 1831 that the painting, "some 8 feet by 5 feet," was on view free of charge in the City Law Courts: "It is a polished work which gives a very favourable impression of the artist, Mr. Duncan…" Duncan was a founding member of the Montreal Society of Artists.

4. A heart-shaped pincushion, wonderfully decorated with hundreds of tiny glass beads and sequins, with the word 'Montreal' picked out in tobacco coloured beads. For the people of Kahnawàke, the glass beads that decorated this souvenir of Montreal were a tangible link between past and present, a means of preserving traditions of craft passed from one generation to the next.

5. The Maple Box, the commemorative gift created by Montreal photographer William Notman for Queen Victoria's son, Albert Edward, the Prince of Wales, who visited Canada in the summer of 1860 to officially open the Victoria bridge, the "eighth wonder of the world." Notman grouped 315 photographs into two portfolios with a presentation bird's-eye maple box for the Prince. Notman understood the promotional possibilities that these photographs represented, and made a duplicate set which he sent to the 1862 International Exhibition in London, where he was awarded a medal "for excellence in an extensive series of photographs."

FIRE

Of all the challenges Montreal and its inhabitants have faced over the centuries – storms, attacks, disease – fire has been perhaps the greatest. Major institutions and whole areas of Montreal have repeatedly burned to the ground in conflagrations on a scale unimaginable today.

Measures to combat fire have included the establishment of a volunteer fire brigade in 1734, construction of a major aqueduct in 1856, and the establishment of a professional fire department in 1863. Following the fire of 1721, stone was adopted as building material, wood shingles and mansard roofs outlawed, and streets widened and straightened.

1721: Hôtel-Dieu hospital catches ablaze when a musket shot fired during a religious procession hits its roof. 138 houses burn, a major loss in a town of only a few thousand people.

1734: A slave sets fire to her mistress's house and the ensuing blaze spreads and engulfs Hôtel-Dieu (which burns for the third time), as well as 46 other houses.

1765: Hot ashes carried to an attic to be used to make soap touch off a major fire that spreads from rooftop to rooftop. Powder kegs also explode and one quarter of the city is destroyed.

1768: A fire starts in a stable near the river and a school, two churches (including the Congrégation de Notre Dame's chapel) and 100 houses are lost.

1849: Rioters set fire to Sainte-Anne market where the United Province of Canada's assembly sat. The building was destroyed; thousands of records housed in the government's libraries and archives burned as well

1851: The "Great Fire" results in the destruction of over 1,000 houses as well as the town's cathedral and episcopal palace, Molson's Brewery and the Hayes Hotel. 10,000 people were rendered homeless (about a sixth of the population) and damage was estimated at 2.5 million dollars.

1910: A water tank fell through the roof of the Montreal Herald newspaper building on St. Jacques Street causing a major fire which killed 32.

1918: The west wing of the Grey Nun's Convent at René Lévesque and Guy burns, killing 53 children in their beds.

1922: City Hall, constructed in 1878, burns almost completely to the ground.

1927: An afternoon fire in the Laurier Palace movie theatre kills 78, most of them children.

1965: A gas explosion in the suburb of LaSalle kills 27; an explosion in the same area in 1956 had killed 7.

1972: The Wagon Wheel, a country and western bar upstairs from the Bluebird Café on Union Avenue downtown, is set ablaze by three men who were denied entry. 37 were killed.

1976: The acrylic outer shell of Buckminster Fuller's geodesic dome, which had served as the US pavilion at Expo 67, burns completely. The 80 m high structure's frame survived and since 1992 has housed the Biosphere.

1988: 500 barrels of PCBs explode in a warehouse in St.-Basile-le-Grand, east of Montreal. A huge cloud of smoke engulfs the town, and 3,000 are forced to evacuate.

Did you know...

that Canada's first Jewish congregation was established in 1768 by Portuguese and Spanish Jews in Montreal?

Take 5 FIVE TWENTIETH CENTURY RIOTS

There have been numerous riots in Montreal over the years. Perhaps the most famous of the 20th century remains the 1955 Richard Riot that broke out in the wake of the suspension of Canadiens' superstar Maurice Richard for the play-offs.

1900: McGill students rampage and attack City Hall, French language newspapers and Laval University on St. Denis Street. The students believed that French Canadians weren't properly supporting Britain's Boer War.

1944: On several occasions, large groups of military personnel clash with zoot suit wearing youths in Montreal and on the South Shore. The most serious incident was when 100 sailors descended upon 60 zoot suiters at the Verdun Dance Pavilion; a full scale brawl ensued that lasted for hours and resulted in numerous arrests and injuries.

1969: A protest against racism goes awry when students trash Sir George Williams (now Concordia) University's Computer Centre and then set it aflame. The protest results in more than two million dollars damage; surrounding streets were blanketed with computer punch cards.

1969: Montreal's "Night of Terror" ensues when 5,000 police officers and fire fighters walk off the job. Rioting and looting occur and a member of the Quebec Provincial Police is killed outside the Murray Hill Limousine garage as taxi drivers attempt to burn it down.

1972: 500 Rolling Stones fans stuck with counterfeit concert tickets demand to be let into the Montreal Forum to see the show. Bottle throwing and scuffling ensue, and two media mobile units are set ablaze. The previous night, dynamite had exploded underneath one of the Stones' equipment vans outside the Forum; new gear had to be flown in from Los Angeles and arrived just before show time.

They Said It

"Montreal has a rare and picturesque scenic beauty; mountain and river and its far horizon give it an unsurpassed interest for the eye. It carries all the romantic charm of its varied history. But for many people its most appealing aspect is that of a great port, one of the greatest in the world and in many senses unique among all the ports of the globe."

– Stephen Leacock from his book *Leacock's Montreal*

MCGILL

McGill University was founded in 1821 and its medical school, Canada's first, was established in 1832. McGill exists thanks to fur trader and merchant James McGill who, on his death, left 46 acres of land and ten thousand pounds for the purposes of establishing a university. A leading research institution, McGill enrolls 33,000 students and has four affiliated teaching hospitals. One of McGill's greatest assets is its campus. "The grounds of McGill University," noted Stephen Leacock, a McGill professor for thirty years, "are beautifully situated in what is, in a sense, the center of Montreal."

Did you know...

that McGill physicist Ernest Rutherford (1871-1937) was a pioneer in the field of radioactivity and nuclear physics? The New Zealand born Rutherford made many of his most significant findings, including the theory of radioactivity and atomic decay, during his nine years at McGill. He moved to Manchester, England in 1907 and was awarded a Nobel Prize in 1908.

GOING MOBILE

The automobile made its first appearance on Montreal streets in late 1899. Seven years later, pedestrian Antoine Toutant became the first person killed by a car in the city. This sad event did nothing to dampen Montrealers' enthusiasm for the automobile, and in 1908 the city hosted its first car race. 5,000 fans descended upon Delorimier Park to watch hotshot Walter Christie set a record by completing one mile (1.6 km) in two minutes and ten seconds.

Nearly a century later, the car still looms large in Montreal. As of 2003, there were 1.84 million cars in Metro Montreal, or 1.23 per dwelling. Montreal has played hosted to a Formula One Grand Prix event on Île Notre Dame since 1978. The circuit is named after Quebec racing great Gilles Villeneuve, who was killed in a 1982 crash in Belgium. The three-day race attracts over 300,000 spectators and is a major tourist draw.

Did you know...

that Canada's first railway opened in 1836? The line linked South Shore La Prairie with Saint-Jean-sur-Richelieu, a distance of 23 km.

Did you know...

that Gibeau Orange Julep at 7700 Decarie Boulevard is a Montreal landmark? The massive orange citrus dates to the 1940s and is open 24 hours daily in the summer months. Along with its signature Orange Julep drink, Gibeau dispenses standard drive-up fare from a small window. The Julep has found favor with generations of Montreal fast food enthusiasts, late night revelers on their way to the suburbs, and 50s enthusiasts.

They Said It

"The houses are all made of grey stone so that the long narrow streets look very dark. What first strikes the stranger's eyes is the white colour of the roofs which are covered with tin while the shutters are lined with sheet iron, as a protection against fire. This method of building conveys an impression of great monotony."

– Theodore Pavie, French Travel Writer, 1833

HOLD THE LINE

Telephone service came to Montreal in 1879 when Dominion Telegraph began marketing the Bell Telephone. Dominion wasn't the only line in town, however; another company, Montreal Telegraph, was selling the Edison telephone. The hitch was that Dominion Telegraph subscribers couldn't call their Montreal Telegraph counterparts, and vice versa.

This unhappy situation turned out to be short lived, and by the end of 1880, the two companies were gone and Boston's National Bell had established a Canadian arm. At that point, Montreal led Canada in telephones with 546; Toronto and Ottawa trailed with 353 and 230

Did you know...

that the Ouimetoscope Theatre on St. Catherine Street East and Montcalm was the first major venue in North America constructed for the purpose of showing motion pictures? The 1,200 seat theatre was the brain child of Montrealer Leo-Ernest Ouimet. It opened in 1907 and ticket prices ranged from 10 to 25 cents. The building is still standing although the auditorium has been abandoned.

respectively. Decades later, Montreal was the site of Canada's first transcontinental telephone conversation. In 1916 a call linked Montreal's Ritz Carlton Hotel and Vancouver's Globe Theatre.

Communications remains important to the Montreal region; Bell Canada Enterprises (BCE) is the area's third largest private sector employer with 60,000 workers. BCE is headquartered in one of Montreal's more spectacular skyscrapers, 1000 de la Gauchetière, and the Montreal Canadiens play nearby at 1260 de la Gauchetière, otherwise known as the Bell Centre.

Source: Bell Canada Enterprises; Globe and Mail.

PUBLIC TRANSPORTATION TIMELINE

- 1861: The Montreal City Passenger Railway Company is created with eight horse powered vehicles running on ten km of track. In the winter months, sleighs were used in place of streetcars.
- 1863: Yearly ridership reaches 1 million.
- 1892: The first streetcar, know as "The Rocket," debuts on Craig Street (now St. Antoine Street).
- 1894: Horses are retired and the system is completely electrified.
- 1905: "Pay as You Enter" practice begins and conductors no longer collect fares.
- 1910: System comprises of 600 cars and 241 km of track. The fare is five cents and 144 million passengers use the network.
- 1919: Buses debut on Bridge Street near the Lachine Canal. Nicknamed "char a bancs" (wagon with benches), they are converted trucks.
- 1925: Regular bus service established.
- 1937: Regular trolley bus service debuts on Beaubien Street.
- 1939: System serves 200 million passengers who ride 929 streetcars, 7 trolley buses and 224 buses.
- 1951: Montreal Transportation Commission is established and has as its mandate modernizing the system, which includes 937 streetcars.
- 1959: Last tram rides the rails and 175 diesel buses are rolled out. The final day of the streetcar is marked by a parade of 15 of the machines, trailed by three brand new buses.
- 1962: Construction begins on the Metro. Plans for a major underground rail system had been discussed as early as 1902.

Did you know...

that running water did not come to Montreal until 1801? Joseph Frobisher was behind the Montreal Water Works Company, which used wood pipes made from hollowed tree trunks to transport water from springs on Mont Royal.

- 1966: Metro debuts; last trolley bus removed from service.
- 1976: Line 1 (Green Line) gets automatic train control.
- 1976-86: Extensions of Metro Line 1 to Honoré-Beaugrand and Angrignon; Extension of Line 2 (Orange Line) to Côte Vertu.
- 1977: First female bus driver.
- 1986-88: Opening and extension of Line 5 (Blue Line).
- 2002: Pilot project in which 155 buses in downtown Montreal run on bio-diesel.
- 2006: The Metro celebrates its 40th birthday and plans are unveiled to replace a number of the aging fleet's cars with newer models.
- 2007: Metro extends to Laval. A new public transit plan recommends reestablishing street car service on high traffic arteries including Park, Mont Royal and Côte-des-Neiges.

Weblinks

Old Montreal

www.vieux.montreal.qc.ca

Historic city Center Old Montreal. Sponsored by the City of Montreal and the province of Quebec, this site has maps, tours, and historical information about Old Montreal.

Discovering Montreal

www.ville.montreal.qc.ca

City of Montreal site with links to local museums, including many devoted to the history of the city and its institutions.

The First People

Recovered stone spear points suggest that people lived in the lower Great Lakes/St. Lawrence lowlands area as early as 11,000 years ago. Artifacts dating from 7,000 to 3,000 years ago include stone tools used for woodworking. Moreover, the presence of knives, fish hooks, awls, beads and pendants made from copper not native to the area suggests that there was a vast trading network that stretched from the Atlantic to the Gulf of Mexico.

From 1,100 years ago to the time of first contact with the Europeans marks the beginning of the tribes and cultures we recognize today. The Mohawk and St. Lawrence Iroquoian lived in an area that included parts of present day Quebec, Ontario and New York State. The region features hardwood forests and is conducive to agriculture. Crops included corn, beans and squash, and First Nations people of the area were among the first in Canada to practice farming. They were sedentary people who supplemented their diet with fishing, hunting and gathering wild plant food.

The term "Iroquoian" refers to those who speak the "Iroquois" language, a group containing several northern Iroquoian tribes including the St. Lawrence Iroquoian, some of whom lived in what is now the

Montreal area. "Iroquois," on the other hand, refers to members of the League of the Iroquois, which contained the Seneca, Cayuga, Onondaga, Oneida and Mohawk tribes.

The St. Lawrence Iroquoian are gone, and the principal concentrations of Mohawks in Quebec live in the Kanesatake Settlement and the Kahnawake Reserve.

CREATION STORY

According to the Iroquois creation myth, before the world was born the Sky People lived on an island that floated above the earth. There was no death or sadness on this floating island, but also no birth. A Sky Woman became pregnant, and her husband, in a fit of anger, tore up the tree that gave the island light. A hole was created and the woman looked down on the water covering the world below. She tumbled through the hole and just before hitting water was caught by birds and carried to the other animals. The animals set about to help the woman, and dug mud from the bottom of the ocean which they piled on the back of Big Turtle, creating North America.

The woman walked onto the land and made stars by sprinkling dust, then she moved on to making the moon and the sun. The Sky Woman gave birth to twins: Sapling who was very kind, and Flint who had a heart of stone. Sapling was behind everything good – plentiful rivers that flowed both ways, boneless fish and nourishing plants. Flint, on the other hand, was a destroyer and only made things that were difficult and hard – thorny bushes and bony fish. Predictably, Flint was responsible for winter, but Sapling was behind spring. Sapling and Flint battled mightily and eventually Flint was vanquished, but did not die. He remained on Big Turtle's back, and his fury is felt every so often in the form of a volcano.

The Iroquois creation story highlights the role that animals, plants and the earth itself play in Iroquois life and culture.

THE THREE SISTERS

The Three Sisters, embodied by corn, beans and squash, are central to Iroquois culture. These foods formed the Iroquois' principal diet, and are thought to have issued from the body of the Sky Woman's daughter. Farming has traditionally been the responsibility of Iroquois women, who devised an ingenious system in which corn, beans, and squash were planted in the same area. The seeds were strategically "interplanted" such that the growth of each crop complemented that of the others.

ENCOUNTER

The earliest European descriptions of Native people in what is now Quebec comes from Jacques Cartier's 1534 diary. Cartier and his men encountered Mi'kmaq in Chaleur Bay, and soon afterwards met a fishing party of St. Lawrence Iroquoians in Gaspé where Cartier erected a nine metre cross at Pointe-Penouille.

Great Peace Treaty of Montreal

On August 4th, 1701, on a field outside of Montreal specially prepared for the event, The Great Peace Treaty, or "Le Grande Paix" was signed by the governor of New France, Louis-Hector de Callière, and the chiefs of 39 First Nations of northeast North America. In addition to the chiefs, over one thousand other First Nations people were in attendance. While Callière had worked for years on improving relations, the signing of the agreement was largely due to the diplomatic work done by the Huron Chief, Kondiaronk, known to the French as "the Rat."

The several day long negotiations wore heavily on the Huron Chief and he fell ill. Nonetheless, Kondiaronk delivered an impassioned two-hour plea to the assembled French and First Nations people. He died the next day, highly honored and praised by all in attendance, and the agreement was signed soon after. Kondiaronk's grave is thought to lie somewhere near Montreal's Place d'Armes.

In the agreement, the French recognized the independent sovereignty of each nation. The treaty is still considered valid today.

They Said It

> *"Will you ever begin to understand the meaning of the very soil beneath your feet? From a grain of sand to a great mountain, all is sacred. Yesterday and tomorrow exist eternally upon this continent. We natives are guardians of this sacred place."*
> – Peter Blue Cloud (1935-), Kahnawake, Quebec-born Mohawk author.

KAHNAWAKE TODAY

- Geographical location: 10 km southwest of Montreal, on the southern shore of Lake Saint-Louis.
- Area: 4,805 hectares
- As of 2006, Kahnawake had 9, 455 total members: 7, 389 residents and 2, 066 non-residents.
- Territory: Reserve of Kahnawake.

KANESATAKE TODAY

- Geographical location: 53 km west of Montreal, on the north shore of the Ottawa River
- Area: 1, 142 hectares
- As of 2006, Kanesatake had 2,017 total members: 1,342 residents and 675 non-residents.
- Territory: Settlement of Kanesatake

Did you know...

that the Montreal Botanical Garden features a First Nations Garden with more than 300 different species of trees, shrubs and grasses? The garden allows visitors to understand the integral role played by plant-life in Native cultures, and includes examples of hardwood forest, conifer forest and northern territories. The garden highlights the importance of plants not just as crops, but also as medicines and in making tools, clothes and building materials.

Bio CHIEF DONNACONA
OF THE ST LAWRENCE IROQUOIAN

Without Chief Donnacona, Jacques Cartier would have been unable to explore and ultimately claim much of New France. Donnacona was chief of a group of St. Lawrence Iroquois who lived in the village of Stadacona, (near contemporary Quebec City). In July of 1534, he and his people were fishing off the Gaspé Peninsula when they encountered Cartier's expedition. Cartier had recently erected a sizeable cross in the area and claimed the land for France.

When the Iroquoian approached Cartier's ships, they were brought aboard and honored with a feast. At this point, either Donnacona agreed or was forced to part with two of his sons, Domagaya and Taignoagny, who were brought with Cartier back to France. When they returned the following year, the two Iroquoian helped Cartier navigate up the St. Lawrence River and then back to Stadacona.

The French spent the winter with the Iroquoian, but relations began to sour when they did not want to participate in Cartier's plan to travel further up the St. Lawrence to the village of Hochelaga, now the island of Montreal.

Cartier left, and when he returned found that the situation had completely deteriorated. Still, Donnacona mollified Cartier by telling him of the riches of the Saguenay region, and providing his men with natural medicines.

Though rightfully distrustful of the French by now, Donnacona and several of his people attended a feast hosted by Cartier. Here Donnacona, his two sons, and seven others were kidnapped and brought back to France. Cartier told the Iroquoian that Donnacona would return bearing gifts from Europe.

Donnacona is said to have been well treated in France, regaling the king and his court with tales from his homeland. However, the chief and all but one of his party died while in France. When Cartier returned to the New World five years later, he told the Iroquoian that Donnacona was alive and well in France and did not wish to return. Agona, who was now chief of the Stadaconans, realized the extent of Cartier's deception, and this set the table for the coming wars between the French and the Iroquois.

All that remains of Donnacona's legacy today is the city of Donnacona, located 40 km west of Quebec City. It is home to the Bowater paper mill, formerly known as Donnacona Paper.

MONTREAL'S ABORIGINAL POPULATION IN THE 21ST CENTURY

According to the 2001 census, the Montreal region's aboriginal population is 11,085 (excluding the Kahnawake reserve which did not participate in the count). Native peoples thus make up less than 0.3% of the population of the Montreal census area, a far lower proportion than prevails in most Canadian cities.

- Montreal Aboriginal employment rate (2001): 68.8%
- Montreal non-Aboriginal employment rate (2001): 79.3%
- Median employment income for all Aboriginal workers (2000): $20,033
- Median employment income for non-Aboriginal workers (2000): $25,216
- Percentage of Aboriginal income received from government transfers: 17%
- Percentage of non-Aboriginal income received from government transfers: 12%
- Low income rate for Aboriginal People (2000): 35.5%
- Low income rate for non-Aboriginals (2000) 21.3%

LANGUAGE OF THE ST. LAWRENCE IROQUOIAN

The following translations were recorded in Cartier's journal from 1545.

Segada: one
Tigneny: two
Asche: three
Honnacon: four
Ouiscon: five
Aggourzy: head
Hegata: eyes
Ahontascon: ears
Escahe: mouth
Esgougay: teeth
Osvache: tongue
Canada: village

THE SAINT LAWRENCE IROQUOIAN

Between the visits of Cartier in 1534 and Champlain in 1603, the St. Lawrence Iroquoian disappeared. Champlain found abandoned villages at Hochelaga and elsewhere along the St. Lawrence River. Some of these lost villages were substantial, and included crop lands as well as up to forty longhouses capable of sheltering 2,000 people.

Why the St. Lawrence Iroquoian vanished is the subject of theory and conjecture. Disease initiated by contact with Cartier's men? Crop failure? Or perhaps warfare with the Hurons or neighboring Mohawk. Surviving members of the tribe were likely assimilated into either the Huron or Mohawk people.

THE LANGUAGE OF THE MOHAWK

Mohawk belongs to the Iroquoian linguistic family and contains three major dialects: Western (Six Nations and Tyendinaga), Central (Ahkwesáhsne) and Eastern (Kahnawake and Kanehsatake). The written form of Mohawk was standardized at the Mohawk Language Standardization Conference held in 1993. In this system, only 12 of the 26 letters of the Roman alphabet are used. The origins of the term Mohawk derives from a combination of two Algonquin words: Mohowawog ("man-eaters") and Mhuweyek ("cannibal-monsters"). In their own language Mohawks refer to themselves as Kanien'keha or "people of the flint."

Did you know...

that during the late 19th Century many Mohawk men began labouring in high risk iron work? The Mohawk built bridges and skyscrapers, first in the Montreal area and subsequently in New York State. Mohawks have worked on many New York City landmarks including the Empire State Building, Rockefeller Center and the World Trade Center.

MOHAWK OF KAHNAWAKE

The early history of the Mohawk in the Montreal region is intertwined with that of Eurocentric missionaries who did not understand Native spiritual traditions, and who felt it was their duty to "Christianize" the so-called pagans. As early as 1667, Father Pierre Raffeix and a group of French families started a mission called La Prairie de la Madeleine.

This mission was moved to several different locations around the St. Lawrence, ending up in 1716 at its current location near the Lachine Rapids, where it became known to the French as Le Mission Sault St. Louis, and as Kahnawake ("At the rapids") to the Mohawk. Though its early native inhabitants were mostly Oneida and Huron, a sizeable Mohawk immigration from what is now New York State resulted in their becoming the area's dominant group.

Oka Crisis

The issues of self-governance, sovereignty and land-claims that were central to the Oka conflict did not originate with Oka, but they were certainly brought to the public's attention as a result of the crisis.

The precipitating event was the proposed expansion of a golf course (whose clubhouse was situated on a historic Mohawk cemetery) onto more Mohawk land. Local Kanesatake residents set up a barricade on the disputed area, and were soon joined by armed members of the Kahnawake and Akwesasne nations, as well as other First Nations people from across the country.

At the same time, Mohawk from Kahnawake blocked the passage through their reserve to Montreal's Mercier Bridge, a major thoroughfare. On June 11, 1990, officers from the Sûreté de Québec attacked the barricade, but were forced to retreat after the death of one of theirs officers. In the tense 78-day standoff, the Sûreté officers were joined by more than 2,000 Canadian troops, the first time since Louis Riel that Canadian soldiers had been dispatched to deal with a conflict with native people.

An agreement was eventually brokered by the Six Nations Iroquois Confederacy, and on August 29, 1990 the Kahnawake Mohawks removed the Mercier Bridge blockade. A month later, the last of the Mohawk warriors surrendered.

MOHAWK OF KANESATAKE

In 1676, Sulpician missionaries established a mission at Mount Royal on the island of Montreal, subsequently moving it to an opening on the Ottawa River. The population was mixed, containing members of Nipissing and Algonquin ancestry, as well as Iroquois. As such, the area is referred to as "Kanesatake," as well as "Oka," which is Algonquin.

In 1945, the federal Department of Indian Affairs purchased the land from the Sulpicians, but did not classify the land as a reserve as the Mohawk had wanted. The transaction embodied a complaint First Nations people have had with the Canadian government – that they may negotiate for them, but rarely do they negotiate with them.

CREATION & SPIRITUAL TRADITIONS

The Iroquois belief system revolves around the Master of Life, or Supreme Being, the most powerful spirit. The Iroquois made little distinction between the natural and supernatural worlds; in this system animals, plants and inanimate objects had souls and spirit beings were always present. To appease the spirits, gifts such as tobacco were left at specific locations. When speaking to the spirits, tobacco leaf was sprinkled on the fire, in the hope that the smoke would help carry the words to the upper world. Contact was also made with spirit beings through ritual fasting, singing, dancing and the ingestion of psychoactive substances.

The Iroquois believed in evil and the existence of demons who threatened humans. They had two methods to combat these demons:

Did you know...

that when Jacques Cartier and his crew fell victim to scurvy, a local Iroquois chief delivered branches of an evergreen tree called annedda, along with instructions on its use? Within days, Cartier's crew recovered, causing him to write, "Had all the doctors of Louvain and Montpellier been there, with all the drugs of Alexandria, they could not have done so much in a year as did this tree in eight days..."

The False Face Society who exorcised evil spirits and drove away disease, and the Secret Medicine Society who existed to give thanks.

Iroquois cultures were matrilineal and clan based. People lived in characteristic long houses, which were large rectangular-shaped buildings designed to house a number of families related to each other on the women's side. If the family grew, so did the longhouse itself. Each individual also belonged to one of the animal clans that were used for ritual purposes, again determined by the mother's clan. When a man married, he moved in with his wife's family. Given this form of social organization, Iroquois women yielded considerable influence at a time when their European counterparts had little power.

Traditionally, Iroquois men hunted, fought, traded and carried out diplomatic missions. The women planted, harvested, gathered firewood and prepared meals; however, when agriculture became more important, the division of labor was adjusted accordingly.

WAMPUM
Wampum beads were woven into belts and given as gifts used to cement agreements with other First Nations people or Europeans.

THE LEAGUE OF IROQUOIS OR SIX NATIONS
The League of the Iroquois, or the Haudenosaunee ("People of the longhouse"), joined together the five separate nations of the Seneca, Cayuga, Onondaga, Oneida and Mohawk some time during the late fifteenth or early sixteenth century. Iroquois oral tradition gives the initial credit for the merger to Deganawidah, who was said to possess supernatural powers.

The alliance was meant to stop inter-tribal warring, and was held together by a constitution known as the Great Law of Peace. While the members of the group continued to pursue their own goals, the league

Did you know...

that Iroquois drums, often made from hollowed-out logs, were frequently filled with water giving them a distinctive and unique sound?

became a powerful political and military alliance that was later joined by the Tuscarora, a group of displaced people from the United States, whose inclusion resulted in the group renaming itself the Six Nations.

IROQUOIS LEGEND: WHY THE BEAR HAS A SHORT TAIL

In the beginning, the bear had a long tail of which he was very proud. One day, a coyote decided to play a trick on the bear. He cut a hole in the ice, and when the curious bear passed by, the coyote told him he was catching fish by dangling his tail into the water. The bear was impressed and asked if he could try.

The coyote said he would watch and tell the bear when to pull his tail out to retrieve the fish, but instead he left the bear and did not come back until the following morning. When he returned, he found the bear had fallen asleep. The coyote woke him and the bear found that his tail was frozen to the ice. In a failed effort to chase after the coyote, the bear ripped his tail from the ice, removing almost all of it. This is why the bear has a short tail.

Weblinks

Montreal Native Friendship Centre

http://www.nfcm.org/

A multi-faceted resource designed to "promote, develop, and enhance the quality of life in the urban Aboriginal community of Montreal."

Quebec Regional Office of Indian and Northern Affairs

http://www.ainc-inac.gc.ca/qc/index_e.html

A comprehensive government-affiliated website covering everything from specific tribal histories to land claims issues.

Mohawks of Kahnawake

http://www.kahnawake.com/

A frequently updated site run by the Mohawk people of Kahnawake.

Go Ahead, Take Five More

As you can probably tell, we are partial to things you can count on one hand. This chapter is more of that. It is designed to be fun, entertaining and insightful, not only in details about the city, but also about the person making the choices. It is a chapter that could have continued well beyond the bounds of this book. Montrealers, famous and not so famous, were literally bursting at the seams with opinions about their city.

TAKE 5: LUC ROBITAILLE'S FIVE REASONS WHY HE LOVED PLAYING HOCKEY IN MONTREAL

Luc Robitaille was born in Montreal in 1966. He played his junior hockey for the Hull, Quebec Olympiques, racking up 425 points in three years. Robitaille made his NHL debut in 1986-87 with the Los Angeles Kings, scoring 45 goals and winning the Calder Trophy as the league's top rookie. In a career spanning 19 years, 14 of them with the Kings, Robitaille netted 668 goals and added 726 assists for 1,394 points. He holds the all-time NHL record for goals and points by a left winger. He is president and co-owner of the Omaha Lancers of the United States Hockey League. Luc Robitaille lives in Los Angeles with his wife, Stacia, a singer, and their two sons.

1. **The Old Montreal Forum.** The Forum was the greatest place to play hockey. It had the best atmosphere, and I loved all the banners hanging from the rafters.

2. **The hot dogs.** Montreal has the best hot dogs in the league ... love the way they toast the buns!

3. **The fans.** Every fan believes he or she has a chance to play in the NHL.

4. **The press.** No city in the world covers hockey as intensely.

5. **The location.** Loved playing so close to my parents and siblings.

TAKE 5: STEPHEN BARRY'S FIVE FAVOURITE PERFORMERS HE HAS SHARED A STAGE WITH

Stephen Barry was born in Lachine, Quebec in 1947 and started playing the blues in the early 1960s. The Stephen Barry Band made its debut at Montreal's Rainbow Bar & Grill in 1975. Since then, the band has toured extensively, including Europe and South America. The Stephen Barry Band plays classic blues, folk-blues and swing. In 1996 the band was named "Blues Group of the Year" by the Toronto magazine *The Jazz Report*. Stephen Barry received a Quebec Lys Blues award in 2004, and a"Bass Player of the Year" award from the Toronto Blues Society in 2001. The band has recorded seven albums, including their most recent, Bluesville.

1. **Bo Diddley** (1978). Three concerts in Montreal. Bo was great and had a great guitar sound. We had a five minute rehearsal. Bo sang a lot of blues.

2. **John Lee Hooker** (1983). When I asked him if he would signal chord changes, he said: "No change." We boogied all night in Quebec City.

3. **Hubert Sumlin** (over a 10-year period in the '80s). He was Howlin' Wolf's guitar player for 35 years; we became friends through the Rising Sun Jazz and Blues Club, where we were the house band. Sumlin was a blues genius and a beautiful player. He is still touring today.

4. **Johnny "Big Moose" Walker** (late '70s-late '80s). A blues piano player from Chicago, he used to say, "Stee, you and me are twins!"although nothing could be further from the truth – I was Northern, white and skinny, and he was Southern, black, big and fat! He was all blues and we had a ball.

5. **Willie Mae "Big Mamma" Thornton** (late '70s-late '80s). The greatest blues singer in the world, she could make the hairs stand up on the back of your neck. She drank gin and milk, a mix she called "tough milk." We were one of the last bands she played with before she died. Big Mama was the Queen of the Blues and wasn't afraid of nobody!

TAKE 5: JIM HYNES' FIVE BEST-KEPT SECRETS ABOUT MONTREAL

A frequent contributor to Canadian travel publications, Jim Hynes is also the consulting editor of this book. He is a freelance writer and book editor born and raised in historic Chambly on Montreal's South Shore. The Montreal neighbourhoods he has lived in include the Plateau Mont-Royal, the Centre-Sud, Ville-Emard, Westmount, and Notre-Dame de-Grace (NDG). The 1993 Stanley Cup Parade started outside his front door.

1. **The St. Leonard Cave:** Legend has it this 10-20,000 year-old rock formation was first used by natives and later as a hideout by Patriotes during the Rebellion of 1837, although there is no evidence to back up either theory. Located in Parc Pie XII in St. Leonard, the 35-metre long, 8-metre deep cave was first discovered early in the 19th century.

The cave is operated by the Borough of St. Leonard together with the Quebec Spelunking Society.

2. Surfing the St. Lawrence: The St. Lawrence River doesn't have huge waves, but it does have fast-moving water, making it popular with enthusiasts of the growing sport of river surfing. The stretch of water around Habitat 67 is particularly suited to ridin' the tide and a number of adventure tour operators now organize river surfing lessons, excursions and equipment rental there.

3. Dufresne Mansion: Located near the intersection of Pie IX and Sherbrooke in the shadow of Olympic Stadium, the Beaux-Arts style palatial home of millionaire shoemakers and future politicians Oscar and Marius Dufresne was built in 1916 by Parisian architect Jules Renard, who used Versailles' Petit Trianon as his inspiration. Today it's a history museum and visual arts centre.

4. Monkland Avenue: This main thoroughfare west of Decarie Boulevard in the Notre-Dame-de-Grace (NDG) district has morphed from a strictly residential street to a mostly commercial one, with many good restaurants, lively bars and pubs, and cute boutiques and shops. Anglo diehards were appalled when the dingy old Monkland Tavern was turned into an upscale, Parisien brasserie-style eatery.

5. Montreal Holocaust Memorial Centre and Museum:
Montreal is home to the third-largest holocaust survivor population in the world. Through their permanent collection of holocaust photos and artifacts, the museum tells an important story to its visitors, and encourages then to fight intolerance in their everyday lives. The museum is located on Côte-Ste-Catherine Road in the Côte-Des-Neiges district.

TAKE 5: ANDRA MCCARTNEY'S TOP FIVE LACHINE CANAL SOUNDS

Andra McCartney is an Associate Professor teaching sound in media for the Communication Studies department at Concordia University. A soundwalk artist, she records ambient sounds in the field, and edits them digitally to create pieces that are evocative of the places recorded. Her works are heard on radio, in gallery installations and online, as well as on several CD anthologies. For the last several years, she has been recording sounds around the Lachine canal, which runs 15 km from Old Montreal to the town of Lachine.

1. **The Rapids.** The Lachine canal was built because of intense rapids in the St. Lawrence River. These can be heard (and viewed!) from the lakeshore in La Salle, but my favourite listening post is Parc René Levesque, between La Salle and Lachine. Here, waves and rivulets of the rapids mingle with ringing of church bells at St. Anne's in Lachine, boats passing by on their way into harbour, whirrs and hums of skaters and cyclists, and laughter of children playing in the park.

2. **The Pier.** Everyone is attracted to the pier: people, fish, boats, swallows, ducks, sparrows, gulls. The island of Montreal is surrounded by the social maritime soundscapes of piers, like in the Old Port, at St. Anne de Bellevue, or in Lachine, where birds nest in the lighthouse eaves. Listen especially in the winter, as ice whispers and groans against the wharves.

3. **Atwater Market**, directly adjacent to the canal, is a favourite soundscape, summer or winter. Here, all my senses are delighted... aromas and flavours of fresh produce, coffee, and cheeses, surrounded by social sounds: voices of vendors and their radios; thumps of produce cases being unloaded; cutlery clinking in cafés.

4. **The Locks.** Compare the soundscape of the Lachine Canal locks with those of the St. Lawrence Seaway on the south shore. Pleasure craft on the Lachine Canal and put-put-putter into the canal, while on the seaway, huge tankers slow the bass roar of their diesel engines as alarms clang. Now try to imagine the Lachine Canal locks in the 1950s filled with blackened steamers, and their horns and whistles.

5. **Griffintown.** For a historical trip, I am fascinated by the sounds of Griffintown as crafted by my student, Lisa Gasior, for her M.A. project in Media Studies. She has recorded many lively interviews with former residents of this immigrant Irish community near the Lachine Canal, and you can listen to them while walking through the streets.

TAKE 5: BERNARD PERUSSE'S FIVE FAVOURITE CONCERT VENUES

Bernard Perusse has been covering the music scene for *The Gazette* for more than a decade, a job that has taken him to venues of all sorts, from seedy nightclubs to hockey arenas. Perusse says the beloved Spectrum, which is set to close at the time of this writing, couldn't be touched when it came to atmosphere, energy and history. There are still several terrific places to see a concert, he says, that don't involve the inevitable sonic brutality of the Bell Centre or the highly-overrated Salle Wilfrid-Pelletier of Place des Arts.

1. **Club Soda** (1225 St. Laurent Blvd.): It's moderately-sized (525 seated, 800 standing) and unassuming, perfect for the artist with a rabid cult following. And when they make the street level a standing-room section, you can bypass it, climb a flight of stairs and get some great seats overlooking the stage — with an unobstructed view of the performer.

2. **Cabaret Juste Pour Rire** (2111 St. Laurent Blvd.): There are fewer rock and pop shows there since it changed ownership in 2006, but the concerts that are still offered in this wonderful club showcase its superb sound and intimacy. With microbrewery beer on tap, all the elements for a perfect evening are in place.

3. **Olympia Theatre** (1004 Ste. Catherine St. E): It's a bit of a hike east from the central club area around Ste. Catherine St. and St. Laurent Blvd., but this 1,300-capacity theatre, in all its seedy, run-down glory, is certainly among the most underused and underrated locations for a rock n' roll show.

4. **Salles du Gesu** (1200 Bleury): This small concert hall's annual high profile during the Montreal International Jazz Festival always reminds us of its clear sound, its hushed magic, and the wonderful late-night listening that can be made available to 425 people.

5. **Kola Note** (5240 Park Ave.): This is where Club Soda used to be located until 1999. Now it's pretty much strictly a world-music venue, but there's something about the highly-electric atmosphere in this 450-capacity club that makes it special.

TAKE 5: PAUL WATERS FIVE FAVOURITE PIECES OF STREET ART
No city can claim to be cultured without decorating its streets and squares with a collection of "public art." That can include everything from war monuments to unintelligible jumbles of steel hoops with pretentious names. Over the last 15 years, Montreal's Bureau d'Art Publique has amassed more than 300 sculptures, installations, paintings and photographs that are displayed in public sites all over the city, 225 of them outdoors. Add to that all the works that civic minded corporations have added to the cityscape and you have quite a collection. Some of it falls into what Tom Wolfe termed "turd in the square" art,

but some of it's quite memorable. We asked Paul Waters, Montreal journalist, editor and travel writer and fancier of all things free (he is Scottish by birth) to pick his five favourites.

1. **La foule Illuminée** (Illuminated Crowd): Even on a sunny afternoon, there's something almost menacing about this huddled horde of waist-high, soap-coloured figures marching across the esplanade in front 1981 McGill College St. The figures in the front are quite bourgeois and respectable; the ones in the back seem caught in the pains of hell. I'm not sure that Franco-British sculptor Raymond Mason succeeded in depicting the degradation of the human species but he sure succeeded in scaring the heck out of me.

2. **Man Reading a Newspaper:** OK, I know this life-size bronze outside a shop on Ste. Catherine St. in Westmount falls into what most critics would dismiss as the dogs-playing-poker school of art, but even a city as sophisticated as Montreal should have room for some whimsical bad taste. Besides, he's reading *The Gazette*, a paper that has helped to keep me and my family well fed.

3. **La Joute (The Joust):** Part puppet show, part fountain, part Johnny Cash song (it has a ring of fire), I like to call this elaborate sculpture-installation by seminal Quebec artist Jean-Paul Riopelle the Muddle in the Puddle. It puts on a 32-minute show every hour with flames, moving metal figures and jets of water. Endlessly entertaining, even if you have no idea what Riopelle was trying to say.

4. **Louis Cyr: Strongman** (1863-1912), who once lifted 4,337 pounds lying on his back, was a pioneering physical-fitness buff and an authentic Québécois hero. This larger-than-life bronze by Quebec artist Robert Pelletier does him full justice. With his arms folded over his burly chest and an old-fashioned dumbbell at his feet, he stands forever at the convergence of St. Jacques and St. Antoine Sts. keeping a steady eye on the working-class district he patrolled as a beat cop.

5. **The Biosphere:** Buckminster Fuller's geodesic dome used to be a building but ever since a fire destroyed its transparent acrylic panels in 1976, leaving just the aluminum structure behind, it can only be called a sculpture — at 268 feet in height, the tallest one in Montreal. As a reminder of that glorious summer of 1967, it manages to be both nostalgic and futuristic at the same time, not to mention, a distinctive part of the city skyline.

TAKE 5: WANDA KALUZNY'S FIVE FAVOURITE THINGS ABOUT MONTREAL

Kaluzny, a native Montrealer, began her conducting career at the age of 11 when she assumed the position of organist and choir director at the Holy Cross Parish. Nine years later she founded the Montreal Chamber Orchestra (MCO) making her the youngest and only woman conductor of a professional orchestra in Canada. In April 1990, she was the first woman to guest conduct the Baden-Baden Symphony in Germany. The Board of Trade of Metropolitan Montreal recognized Kaluzny as "a woman whose life is synonymous with commitment and success." Kaluzny can be heard in concert with the Montreal Chamber Orchestra at Salle Claude-Champagne.

1. **Favourite neighbourhood: Mile-End.** I've lived in various parts of the city but Mile-End continues to be my favourite because of its wonderful diversity.

2. **Favourite concert hall: Salle Claude Champagne.** I attended concerts in this hall since I was a teenager and it has always been a favourite of mine. The acoustics are fabulous (my favourite place to sit is in the balcony) and I am delighted that the Montreal Chamber Orchestra moved its performances to Salle Claude-Champagne in 2005.

3. **Favourite lunch spot: Le Parchemin.** I love this place for its food and ambiance but also because it occupies the building where the choir from Christ Church used to rehearse. As a student, I would often join the choir when they were performing large works and it's fun to be sitting in the same place, albeit in a completely different role.

4. **Favourite way to relax:** taking walks on the mountain with my dog Daisy.

5. **Favourite place to people watch:** breakfast at Café Souvenir.

TAKE 5: BILL HAUGLAND'S 5 MOST MEMORABLE STORIES HE'S COVERED

Bill Haugland was born in Montreal in 1942 and attended Macdonald High School in Ste-Anne-de-Bellevue, where he was a gymnast and aspiring Olympian. When he was 19 his father wangled him an interview with Gord Sinclair Jr. of CFOX radio in Pointe Claire. He studied broadcasting at Toronto's Ryerson University and started his career at CFCF Television (now CTV Montreal) in 1961 when he took a job in the mailroom. He moved up through the ranks and eventually assumed anchor duties in 1977, a post he held until his retirement in late 2006.

1. **Monsanto chemical explosion.** LaSalle, Quebec, October 12, 1966. I stood for several hours beside a chemical tank, surrounded by a raging fire. The tank was being sprayed by firemen, who later advised me that if the chemical it contained had reached its flashpoint and exploded, it would have taken out a four square mile area. Whew!

2. **School bus level-crossing tragedy.** Dorion, Quebec, October 7, 1966. If ever there was instilled in this then young reporter a sense of tragedy, it was standing amidst row upon row of small, white caskets at the funeral of the students whose school bus was hit by a CN freight train at a Dorion level-crossing. Nineteen were killed instantly. It provoked a new focus on rail level-crossing safety in Quebec.

3. **McGill University en français riot.** March 28, 1969. Ten-thousand trade unionists, leftist activists and CEGEP students went on a rampage at McGill's Roddick gates. Demonstrators saw McGill as a bastion of Anglophone privilege in a predominantly French city.

4. **Lennon bed-in. May 26, 1969.** John and Yoko in bed, in room 1742 at the Queen Elizabeth Hotel. I interviewed the famous couple, and came away wondering how lying in bed could end the fighting and further the peace ideal. War continued, but the Lennon legend was being established.

5. **James Cross kidnapping.** Cross was freed by FLQ captors on December 3, 1970. I saw the windowless room in which the British diplomat, then Britain's Senior Trade Commissioner in Montreal, had been imprisoned for more than two months.

TAKE 5: RONALD STEWART AND WILLIAM HENSON'S FIVE REASONS MONTREAL IS SUSCEPTIBLE TO ICE STORMS

Ronald Stewart, Ph.D., and William Henson, Ph.D., are members of the Extreme Weather Group in McGill University's Department of Atmospheric and Oceanic Sciences. The Extreme Weather Group is devoted to studying extreme weather events and trends, including droughts and ice storms. Dr. Stewart and Dr. Henson have authored several articles appearing in atmospheric science journals on the subject of the Montreal ice storm of 1998.

1. The long winter season means that there is a large window in which ideal ice storm conditions can occur.

2. Montreal is far enough north that it is quite often below freezing in winter, but far enough south that it's not too frigid.

3. Montreal lies in the track of major winter storms that bring warm air from the south and produce large amounts of precipitation.

4. The Montreal area lies in the St. Lawrence River Valley, which can trap cold air, prolonging the conditions for freezing rain.

5. Warm air from the south can descend the Appalachians and warm further, enhancing the conditions for freezing rain. The warm air then rises and cools over the Laurentians, promoting production of snow and/or ice pellets.